# COLLECTOR'S GUIDE TO
# TREASURES FROM THE
# SILVER SCREEN

# Wallace-Homestead Collector's Guide™ Series

Harry L. Rinker, Series Editor

Collector's Guide to American Toy Trains, by Al and Susan Bagdade
Collector's Guide to Autographs, by Helen Sanders, George Sanders, and Ralph Roberts
Collector's Guide to Baseball Cards, by Troy Kirk
Collector's Guide to Comic Books, by John Hegenberger
Collector's Guide to Early Photographs, by O. Henry Mace
Collector's Guide to Quilts, by Suzy McLennan Anderson
Collector's Guide to Toys, Games, and Puzzles, by Harry L. Rinker
Collector's Guide to Treasures from the Silver Screen, by John Hegenberger
Collector's Guide to Victoriana, by O. Henry Mace

# Contents

# Foreword

Surrounded by wall-to-wall bookshelves (all film books, of course) and files of stills, posters, and pressbooks, plus more shelves (and closets) full of 16mm prints, I do not consider myself a *collector*. Perhaps it's because I teach film history and feel the need to be objective, keeping history separate from nostalgia. Perhaps, too, it is because collecting in the film area has now become a rich man's game. I find it almost obscene that in today's market an original movie poster can often command a price twenty times the price for a print of the film itself. I've even seen some posters priced higher than the *budget* for the original film. But although I tell myself that all my artifacts are tools for my work, obviously I *am* a collector, and wouldn't have missed the thrill of the chase after stills or posters when I was a youngster at school—when pennies for puchases had to come out of meager savings or be purloined from lunch money.

I grew up in England in the early thirties, when film books were vitrually nonexistent. Collectibles then consisted largely of merchandising tie-ins; circulation-building free gifts in film magazines (usually postcards); cigarette cards (about one series in twelve devoted to movies); souvenir programs for major films; and so forth. These were usually easy enough to obtain, and only the cigarette cards relied on stamina and chance. One had to watch for an adult to throw away the empty cigarette carton in the street and then pounce, hoping it would still contain the card. Usually it did, since smokers themselves seemed to have little interest in collecting. Some of the cards were truly beautiful, all shapes and sizes and themes—though it was frustrating to want only movie cards and constantly to salvage Kings and Queens or Wild Life!

The cigarette companies promoted collecting by issuing albums with appropriate framings for the cards and short identifying notes beneath each one. (Most British companies selling products that might get into the hands of children—cocoa, for example— used free gift "come-ons" as well, though the giveaways were usually non-film-oriented: tin soldiers or animals that seemed to retain their cocoa aroma for a lifetime!) I amassed quite a collection of cigarette-card books on filmic themes and was very proud of them. During the early days of the war, however, I was inspired by one of Winston Churchill's most eloquent "give till it hurts" speeches, tied in with a salvage drive, and since I was still too young to contribute greatly to the war effort, decided to turn in all my albums. Feeling very patriotic, I had all my good intentions dashed when the unfeeling Salvage Warden said, "Oh, we won't throw *these* away—my little boy would like them!" I should have retrieved them on the spot, but I hope whichever little boy got them was a potential Kevin Brownlow who kept them and still has them. Framed single pages of those albums now fetch a small fortune, but usually a *reasonable* small fortune, so that collectors tend to buy them at conventions as Christmas presents for other collectors. I was presented with one such, from a 1935 album, and it is now displayed right below an original Churchill wartime poster!

While the easily obtained souvenir programs were nice to have, like most collectors I was more excited by something unique, preferably by something that had a kind of "inside" connection to the film industry—namely, posters, pressbooks, and stills. In England (and in America too) these were not so easy to obtain, since most publicity material was controlled by one company, National Screen Service, which also made the "coming attraction" trailers. They leased stills and posters to exhibitors for a nominal amount and got them back after the showing for recirculation. I frequently cajoled and pleaded with exhibitors to sell me the stills they displayed so enticingly and was never once successful. Pressbooks were something else again: they were in plentiful supply, were given away free, and one or two exhibitors who admired my enthusiasm gave me batches of these periodically. It was a tremendous thrill to read through them, enjoy all the publicity stories (packs of lies though most of them were) and to pick up a lot of trade jargon. One of the first pressbooks that I thus obtained was an elaborate one for the 1936 British Cary Grant film, *The Amazing Quest of Ernest Bliss*. I still have it, in excellent condition, and it makes a useful display-case artifact when I show the film, as I often do, in film history series at such institutions as Berkeley's Pacific Film Archive.

With stills-for-collectors such a flourishing and well-organized business now, it's hard to believe that at one time acquiring stills was a real coup. They did sometimes show up in small batches in secondhand bookshops. And luckily they were reasonably priced in the thirties, when the collecting field was still small. Usually when one found a little cache, one would buy them all, regardless of content. If there were one or two desirable ones then they were a pleasant bonus—but just having glossy stills was an achievement in itself. I have many stills in my own collection from exceedingly dull or unimportant movies, many of which do not even show the lead players. Officially, I keep them against the day when one particular still might suddenly be needed and unavailable elsewhere; but, to be honest, I keep them more to remind myself how grateful we were for *anything* in the earlier days of collecting. In wartime England, glossy stills were banned because the armed forces needed all the photographic material, and stills for exhibitors were printed on lackluster nonsensitized paper. 20th Century Fox even printed *color* stills on a kind of coarse cardboard: Betty Grable *never* looked less attractive, but even these have a kind of academic collecting value.

Once I was old enough to wear long trousers (in many schools, it was forbidden until one reached the age of 16) and to start a little film review column in my local paper, I was able to "prove" I was a journalist and thus was able to assail the National Screen Service archives in England and obtain pressbooks and stills for press purposes. Since most of what I wanted was old and not likely to be needed again, my credentials were never questioned, and most of the time I was not even charged. A smaller, similar company in London called Girosign had a process whereby they daubed washes of colored paint on the backs of stills. The idea was for them to be displayed in still cases where electric lights *behind* the stills would turn them into color stills. Considering the apparent casual application of paint, the results are quite striking; American collectors, unfamiliar with the process, are often amazed when they see the effectiveness of such a simple idea.

Collecting film magazines in England was as easy as it must have been here: there were just so many of them. England had at least four major weekly fan magazines, all of them with high standards, and all publishing periodic holiday special issues. In addition, the more erudite *Sight and Sound,* the still extant British Film Institute magazine, was available, as were most American fan magazines, usually for the same price as American comic books, which happened also to be the price of the average chocolate bar. Clearly young British collectors had to make major decisions.

Oddly enough, there wasn't too much demand for American fan magazines, possibly because distribution was erratic and continuity therefore problematic. Sooner or later they turned up in secondhand bookshops, where they could be bought cheaply. One of the best in London was an incredibly dirty and overstocked little shop in Ealing called Lamb's. It was more warehouse than shop, and how purchasers could even get *into* the shop over its piles of books and magazines was something of a mystery. But one of my favorite childhood pastimes was cycling to Ealing after I got out of school, detouring past the pleasant, relaxed front of Ealing Studios, and down to Lamb's. After that I had a six-mile cycle home, with piles of film magazines strapped to the back of the cycle and balanced on the handlebars. Since I had started collecting movie magazines *before* I could read, awaiting the day when their treasures would be unlocked to me (they probably accelerated my learning), I never did fully catch up on my backlog.

One of the treasures most sought after in England was an American magazine brought out in the late thirties called *Movie Comics.* Each issue told the stories of several contemporary movies, but entirely via stills with balloon captions. Most of the stories were action-oriented: *Gunga Din,* westerns, *Son of Frankenstein,* the latter particularly titillating to a British youth, since film censorship banned the film to anyone under 16. Some of the movies were curiously chosen; *The Great Man Votes,* for example, depended on a witty script and fine acting, qualities that did not translate well into a pictorial synopsis. On the other hand, its inclusion was a kind of endorsement, and many English youngsters went to see worthwhile films they might otherwise have scorned, purely because they were represented in *Movie Comics.*

Whatever happened to the comic I don't know. It disappeared in England at the end of 1939, when the war made importation an unnecessary luxury. But in all the movie and comic book conventions I have attended in the United States, I have never once seen a single copy for sale. Was it simply forgotten, or has the brevity of its life span made it such a collector's item that it never gets into the hands of dealers?

Britain had a rough (and superior) equivalent in a magazine called *Boy's Cinema;* working from official scripts, it offered two or three in-depth film stories per issue, plus a serial, a smattering of stills, and a page of film news. At a time when there were few ways to see reissues of old films (no TV or videotapes, of course), *Boy's Cinema* was the only means by which one could relive and enjoy old movie favorites. Copies were reread constantly, which accounts for the rather dog-eared quality of those that show up in the collectors' market today. Through the years, I built up a virtually complete collection, going back to the twenties and carrying right through the thirties into its last issues in the very early forties, when wartime paper shortages sounded the death knell for so many magazines. (The four major British fan magazines survived by doubling up, two papers linked in one issue, and at a fraction of the newsprint formerly used.)

When I came to the United States in late 1950, my entire *Boy's Cinema* collection came with me aboard the Queen Mary—and somehow got lost en route. Unpacking on arrival, my discovery that the *Boy's Cinema* box was missing produced emotions akin to those of Sydney Greenstreet when he finds that his long coveted Falcon is a fake. It took the zest out of the whole idea of collecting. Later, however, I began to reconstitute my *Boy's Cinema* collection in a small way and found that while they had served an admirable purpose in my youth, they just weren't as good as I remembered. Dialogue was often changed outrageously into the British idiom, some elements were tactfully censored, and when there was a space problem, complete subplots might be dropped, or an abrupt ending contrived. (I can think of no excuse for such ploys.) While some of the articles can now be seen as sheer puffery, the reviews remain, the ads, the colorful art covers, and all the other elements that make film magazines useful history as well as enjoyable nostalgia. And the prices they fetch these days have spiraled so high that the chances of finding them again at prices one can afford are so slight that one tends to keep everything! A good case in point are the simple, illustrated souvenirs of films that used to be virtually given away in theaters in Europe in the thirties. (The practice never caught on over here.) In England they were called Cinegrams; in Germany, *The Illustrated Film Courier.* The English ones ran to about ten pages, the German ones four to six (but they were larger pages), and most European countries had variations. Their format was simple: stills, an outline of story, cast and credits, maybe a few biographical details. No publicity puffery, no plugs for coming films, just a simple record of the film. In England they sold for one penny apiece in the theaters showing the film. Now when you can find them, the least of them sells for the equivalent of ten dollars; if a big name star or a famous film is involved, it'll be doubled.

I have stopped being a collector (though my wife would dispute that, and the appearance of my apartment would repudiate it) for two reasons. One, and I realize I am extremely lucky and unusual in this respect, it became too easy. I worked in the film industry here and in England for many years and made useful contacts. Then, when I began to do academic work in film history and at film festivals, I made more contacts.

Huge collections of stills are often donated to academic institutions, as are artifacts (such as one of the camera-slates from Griffith's 1924 *America*) and, more and more, collections of film, which I usually rechannel to archives. When you're presented with two or three films that you *might* be able to acquire, the collector instinct boils to the surface. When you're suddenly the inheritor of a collection of a thousand feature films, you become more like a bank teller surrounded by thousands of dollars which are meaningless. Second, collecting has now become big business, usually in the hands of people who know what an item is worth, but have absolutely no love for or knowledge of film and who make the most horrendous claims for their material through sheer ignorance. At many a dealer convention I've seen someone offering a poster as a "mint original" from its premiere release, when the words "a rerelease" are clearly printed on the poster, taking about 15 years off its age and removing two-thirds of its value.

Posters are a particular problem in today's market. Many of them are superbly designed, valuable and interesting for their own sake, not just to collectors of movie nostalgia. Yet the prices they command are so indecent that bona fide collectors can rarely afford them: after all, when the price asked for a poster could buy ten to twenty 16mm prints, there's something wrong. Posters now tend to be sold from dealer to dealer, rather than from dealer to customer. I have a fairly large collection of posters, which I keep partly because I like them. Most important, though, if I have the film itself in my collection, an original artifact showing the way the film was merchandised at the time, as well as the pictorial style of its period, is a useful and educational display adjunct when I show the film at an archive in Berkeley or Zurich. Otherwise, although one or two key posters are framed, most of them reside in drawers. In many cases, I'd be much happier to see them with collectors who would *really* appreciate them. Yet the prevailing market makes it foolish to give them away.

Once in a while a happy solution comes along. A few years ago a collector suddenly noticed my original one-sheet for *King Kong* and offered $10,000 for it. (He was honest enough to admit that I could undoubtedly get more if I put it on the open market.) Now this was a poster I'd bought years ago for 25¢, and the price was still marked on the back. If I accepted his offer, I would be like the dealers I was always condemning. If I refused—and he *really* wanted the poster for its own sake and not for resale—I'd have felt like an idiot and also disappointed him. My initial inclination was to keep the poster, which I liked, and avoid all the moral issues involved. Then a happy solution presented itself: he had a 16mm print of a quite rare film that I was keen to acquire. It had been *given* to him, and he had no interest in it. Even though he felt he was taking advantage of me, it became the ideal compromise. We traded my poster for his film. We each felt that we had gotten by far the better of the deal; on paper, thousands of dollars had changed hands, yet in actual fact my initial 25¢ was the only hard cash involved.

If I have rambled, it is because the whole art of collecting is a lifelong ramble. I look forward to the publication of John Hegenberger's book and am prepared to have him turn me back into a bonafide collector!

William K. Everson

# Acknowledgments

I am indebted to the following people and companies for their help in developing this book:

The major motion picture studios and publishers of film-related subject matter;

Harry Rinker, Kathy Conover, and the late Alan Turner of Chilton Book Company;

John Stingley for excellent photography and insight;

The CINEVENT Committee and Bill Everson for additional assistance;

Camden House Auctioneers for photography and information support;

My wife, Suzie, and kids, Laura, Molly, and John W. Hegenberger, for leaving Dad enough time to write;

My father, John N. Hegenberger, for driving me to the theater all those Saturday afternoons when I was young. Top of the world, Dad!

# CHAPTER 1

# How This Book Can Help You

COLLECTING MOVIE MEMORABILIA is one of the easiest, most popular, and most rewarding pastimes in the world. When I first started collecting movie memorabilia there was no one to show me the way—no one to tell me where to find old movie posters and memorabilia, how to store these treasures, or who would ever want to trade or buy them. There was only the powerful yearning to own a part of the dreams and fantasies of Hollywood, to make them seem more real by making them mine.

If you share in this powerful yearning, then *Collector's Guide to Treasures from the Silver Screen* is your ticket to the fascinating world of motion-picture collectibles, as well as a guide for investing and for valuation. This book is designed to tell you the best way to find and buy Hollywood collectibles, how to take care of them, and, finally, how to sell them so you can afford to go out and collect more.

*Collector's Guide to Treasures from the Silver Screen* can help you find and recognize bargains and help you avoid buying overpriced items. (However, don't let this guide take the fun out of your collecting. Above all, maintain your sense of enjoyment, be true to your own sense of value concerning movie memories—and remember that prices fluctuate.) Many great and wonderful rewards are available to you, once you've learned the best and most affordable ways of creating and adding to a collection of movie material.

First and foremost, this book is full of inside information and little-known tricks that can help you gain more fun from your collection. This book will tell you why collecting movie memorabilia is so popular, entertaining, and easy. It will also tell you a little about yourself and your fellow collectors. If you are already a collector with lots of items, this book can offer you important tips you may not have encountered elsewhere, some of which may surprise you. If you are a new collector, this book offers you a clear, accurate, and thorough picture of the world of movie memorabilia.

The phenomenon of motion pictures is an enormous and influential one, a key part of the hugely successful entertainment industry in America. The history of movies spans

1

a hundred years of combined efforts by top professionals from the fields of design, writing, advertising, acting, music, costuming, set direction, photography, promotion, and packaging, to name a few. These efforts are further interwoven with the careers of world-famous motion-picture stars and directors. Thus, interest in one aspect of movies begets interest in another—and another. For example, if you like actress Myrna Loy from all those *Thin Man* movies, or actor Warner Baxter from the *Crime Doctor* films, you'll want to see *Broadway Bill* (1934), directed by Academy Award winner Frank Capra, which features both Loy and Baxter. And if you decide you like the directing of Capra, you'll want to see his remake of the film *Riding High* (1950), starring Bing Crosby. Or you may wish to see the remake because you are a Bing Crosby fan or because you are a Laurel and Hardy fan and you want to see Oliver Hardy's last feature cameo appearance. And round and round.

Today's movies are major media events created by multimillion-dollar corporations. But this wasn't always the case. Movies began about a hundred years ago with the invention of the motion-picture camera. Some way the Lumière brothers, two Frenchmen, may have invented the first movie camera, but it was Thomas Edison's version that proved to be most practical in America. Pictures were shown in penny arcades, in a machine that the viewer cranked by hand. Later, movies began to be shown on screens in stores and halls where seats had been installed. The admission price was a nickel— hence the term *nickelodeon*.

Business was brisk for this new form of popular entertainment. The public just couldn't seem to get enough of it. Competition to produce and deliver "flickers" to the theaters was intense. In order to escape legal battles and court action instituted by Edison, who held the original patents on the moving-picture machine, many early film pioneers went West to what later became Hollywood, "Home of the Stars."

Encouraged by the frequently sunny weather of southern California, more and more companies—such as Kalem, Biograph, and Selig Studios—began paying wages and creating work in this new, exciting industry on the West coast. In 1912, businessman Carl Laemmle formed the Universal Film Manufacturing Company. The Vitagraph Company had opened for business in Hollywood the year before, and Quality Pictures with its star Francis X. Bushman set up moviemaking in 1915.

In a short time, audiences began to find favorites among the actors and actresses who appeared on the screen. At first, the names of the players were not even mentioned, but gradually favorite performers were given bigger and bigger parts and their names were advertised more than the pictures they played in. Thus, the movie star was born. Giants of the silent era included Charlie Chaplin; Rudolph Valentino; Janet Gaynor; Lon Chaney, Sr.; William S. Hart; Rin Tin Tin; Mary Pickford; Buster Keaton (See Fig. 1-4); and Douglas Fairbanks, Sr.

On October 6, 1927, Al Jolson spoke and sang in the *The Jazz Singer,* and panic shook Hollywood as the sound ear began. Within a few short years, a whole new galaxy of stars began appearing and speaking in "talkies"—stars like Gary Cooper, Greta Garbo, Clark Gable, Mickey Mouse, Mae West, and the Marx Brothers.

2

**Fig. 1-1.** Judy Garland poster for *The Harvey Girls,* a typical MGM musical from the 1940s.

**Fig. 1-2.** Matted sepia portrait still of Errol Flynn by Scotty Welbourne; 8″ × 10″.

By the early 1930s, the studio system was firmly entrenched in the film industry. Major studios like MGM (Metro-Goldwyn-Mayer), Paramount, Warner Brothers, and Fox owned a star's contract and told the performer what films to appear in. Moviegoers hoping to forget their troubles during the Depression rushed to the theater to watch gangster pictures, like *Little Caesar* and *Public Enemy;* horror movies, like *Dracula* and *Frankenstein;* and musicals, like *Top Hat* and *Gold Diggers of 1935*. In time, more and more films were produced in Technicolor, leading to the year 1939, which saw the release of three of the greatest classics: *The Wizard of Oz, Gone With the Wind,* and *The Little Princess*.

**Fig. 1-3.** Autographed black-and-white still of George Reeves as Superman and Robert Shayne as Inspector Henderson; 8″ × 10″.

**Fig. 1-4.** Lobby card from Buster Keaton's 1924 hit *The Navigator*, directed by Donald Crisp for MGM.

**Fig. 1-5.** Poster for *Woman of the Year* (1942), the first pairing of Spencer Tracy and Katharine Hepburn; 41″ × 27″.

Available for viewing besides these grade A movies were a host of budget, or B, pictures. Some studios, like Republic and Monogram, specialized in the low-cost western and serial, while other budget films were produced independently.

After World War II, the Supreme Court changed the course of motion-picture history by declaring in 1948 that the studio system violated antitrust laws. This gave the independent producers a shot in the arm, but it threw the major studios into chaos. Then another technological phenomenon took away a portion of the Hollywood studios' audiences—*television*. Instead of going to the movies, people sat at home and watched the pale blue fire in their TV sets. Desperate, the motion-picture industry tried to find a way to get people back into the theaters. Screens got wider, sound got better, and—briefly—3-D movies seemed more realistic. For more than a decade, the movie industry fought against television, not realizing that it was an ally.

By the mid-1960s, people who had watched the early black-and-white films of Humphrey Bogart, Clark Gable, Joan Crawford, Boris Karloff, Fred Astaire, Greta Garbo, Spencer Tracy, and James Cagney on the intimate late-late show began to regard them as old favorites—classics of Hollywood entertainment. Revival houses began to play to this growing audience. Conventions sprang up almost overnight, as fans of film across the nation gathered to buy, sell, and trade artifacts and memorabilia from the golden days of Hollywood. Museums began to hold retrospectives of the great directors, like Hitchcock, Griffith, Ford, and von Sternberg. Young film students paid homage to earlier works, as in Brian DePalma's *Obsession,* George Lucas's *Indiana Jones* series.

Today, movies are big business, branching out to other forms of communication. Posters, novelizations, teaser ads, and soundtrack recordings are not new; what is, is the fact that each of these media (and more) represents its own big business, producing movie memorabilia collected by fans all over the world. Clearly, movies are all around us. And collecting movie material is one of the most popular of hobbies.

Practically everyone in America has at least one piece of movie memorabilia in his or her possession: a photograph, an autograph, a toy, a book, a record album, or a videotape. Movies and movie memorabilia have touched our lives, reminding us of an emotional moment, a stunning special effect, or the larger-than-life feeling of the success and glory of Hollywood's past.

There are three newspapers—*Movie Collector's World, Big Reel,* and *Classic Images*—generating hundreds of pages each month that concern the collecting of movie material. Hundreds of collectible shops in every major U.S. city feature movie posters, lobby cards, soundtracks, and other memorabilia for even the casual collector. And the serious collector can bid in person or by mail on rare and unique items—such as Superman's uniform or the piano used in Casablanca—at one of the many Golden Age Movie Memorabilia auctions held each year in Los Angeles and New York City.

Yes, there is a wealth of affordable movie material still available to you, if you become knowledgeable and realistic about the marketplace. You may not find collectibles from your favorite movies at first, but you can often exchange what you have for something else. You can always aim for the item of your dreams, and while you seek after it you can learn more about other types of movie collectibles along the way.

**Fig. 1-6.** Bathing suit worn by Esther Williams in *Bathing Beauty* (1944). Esther also posed in this suit for the April 17, 1944, issue of *Life* magazine.

Fig. 1-7. Lobby card from *The Man from Laramie,* autographed by James Stewart.

Fig. 1-8. Original soundtrack recording from *Torn Curtain* (1966). Director Hitchcock is featured almost as prominently as his stars Paul Newman and Julie Andrews, even on the record album.

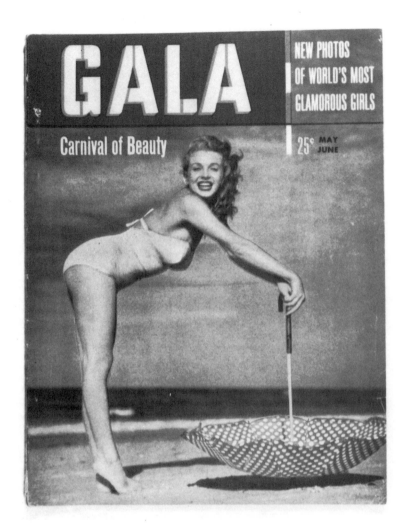

**Fig. 1-9.** *Gala* magazine with cover and interior photos of Marilyn Monroe (vol. 1, no. 1, 1950).

This book is your guide to getting into the movie collectibles hobby and keeping ahead of changes. It presents detailed information on collecting six of the most popular types of movie memorabilia:

Posters, lobby cards, and stills
Books, scripts, and comics
Movie magazines, programs, and press books
Soundtracks
Autographs, Costumes, and cels
Films and videos

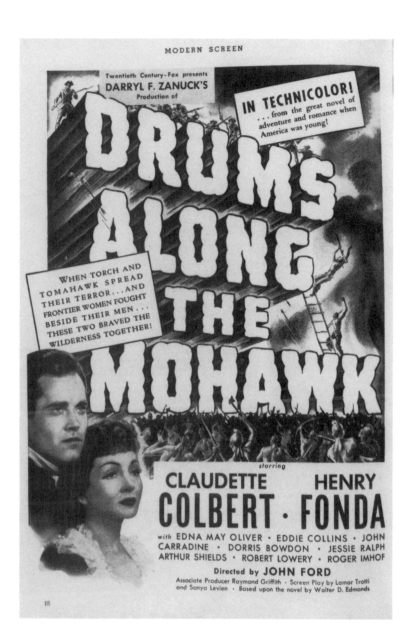

Fig. 1-10. Magazine ad for *Drums Along the Mohawk* (1939), an early John Ford western. Note the prominent promotion of the then-new Technicolor.

**Fig. 1-11.** Linen-backed insert poster for *His Girl Friday* (1939); 11″ × 36″.

Fig. 1-12. A selection of unusual movie magazines. *American Cinematographer* and *Film Comment* are serious publications devoted to the advancement of film art and craft; *Famous Monsters* is equally serious about its subject matter.

The information contained here has developed slowly over many years, partly as a result of my own experience and partly from interviews and discussions with people who've bought, sold, traded, collected, and produced movie memorabilia for decades. I saw a need for a book such as this because I found, over and over, that much of the important nuts-and-bolts information that collectors needed simply wasn't available to them. I found, too, that some of the information used widely among collectors was inaccurate, misleading, and sometimes downright false.

Naturally, everyone has a favorite star or movie. Not every item of this popular and varied hobby can be included in this volume, but the intent is to present what is most typical in order to suggest the basic structure of collecting for you to build on. And remember that the prices quoted in this guide are only that—guides—and are based on prices current at the time of publication.

Because of the enormous amount of activity in this field, plus all the new movie material turned up each year, *Collector's Guide to Treasures from the Silver Screen* will need to be updated from time to time. If you have any suggestions for additions or changes I would like to hear from you by mail. Please write to me in care of Wallace-Homestead Books, Chilton Way, Radnor, PA 19089.

It is my hope that this guide will help to advance your collecting skills and enhance your enjoyment of the hobby.

**Fig. 1-13.** Magazine ad for *Living in a Big Way* (1947). In this film you can watch Gene Kelly's feet or Marie McDonald's body.

**Fig. 1-14.** Part of a press kit to promote the *Deadwood Dick* (1940) serial. Items like this were designed to fit right into the local newspaper's movie or comics pages.

**Fig. 1-15.** Stunning design for magazine ad of *The Sea of Grass* (1947). This ad makes it hard to tell that this film is a western.

**Fig. 1-16.** Magazine ad for *Swing Time* (1936), a four-star Fred and Ginger fest with Oscar-winning tune "The Way You Look Tonight."

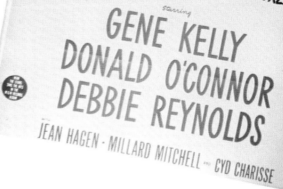

One-sheet poster from *The Phantom of the Opera* (1943).

One-sheet poster from *Singin' in the Rain* (1952).

*Photoplay* (December 1923) featured Constance Talmadge; *Motion Picture*'s cover girl was Rita Hayworth (May 1948); *Movie Classic* featured Gwili Andre (October 1932); Josephine Hutchinson was *Screen Play*'s selection for the October 1936 issue.

*Hollywood* issues featured Gene Tierney (September 1942), and a painting of Gary Cooper and Sigrid Gurie from the 1938 movie *The Adventures of Marco Polo* (December 1937). Janet Blair was the cover girl for *Screen Stars* issue (January 1947) and Linda Darnell was featured on the December 1944 cover.

Lobby card from *King of Kings* (1927).

Lobby card from *The Road to Morocco* (1942) with Bob Hope and Bing Crosby.

Interior view of The Ohio Theatre movie palace as it appears today in Columbus, Ohio. The theater was originally constructed in 1927.

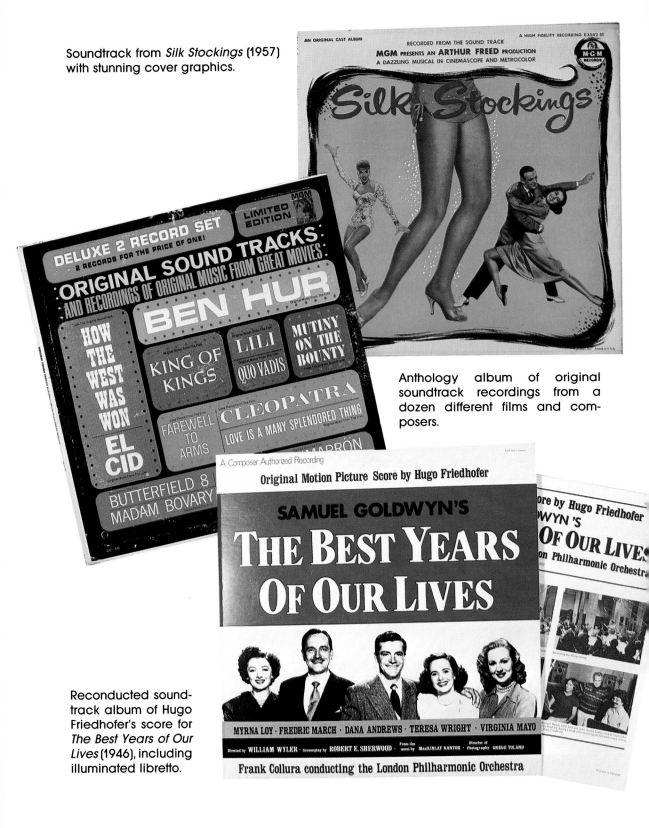

Soundtrack from *Silk Stockings* (1957) with stunning cover graphics.

Anthology album of original soundtrack recordings from a dozen different films and composers.

Reconducted soundtrack album of Hugo Friedhofer's score for *The Best Years of Our Lives* (1946), including illuminated libretto.

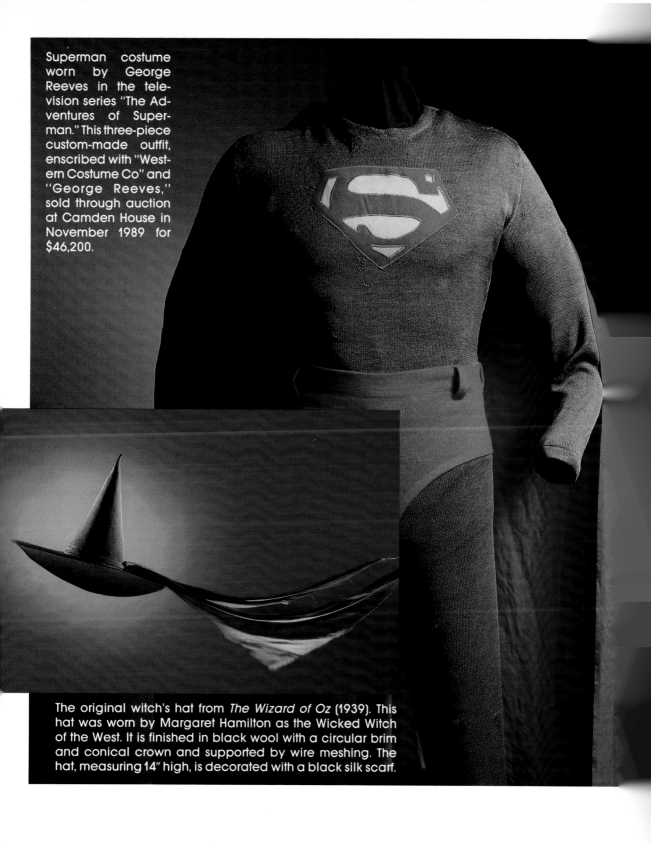

Superman costume worn by George Reeves in the television series "The Adventures of Superman." This three-piece custom-made outfit, enscribed with "Western Costume Co" and "George Reeves," sold through auction at Camden House in November 1989 for $46,200.

The original witch's hat from *The Wizard of Oz* (1939). This hat was worn by Margaret Hamilton as the Wicked Witch of the West. It is finished in black wool with a circular brim and conical crown and supported by wire meshing. The hat, measuring 14″ high, is decorated with a black silk scarf.

One-sheet poster from *Dial M for Murder* (1955), a 3-D movie.

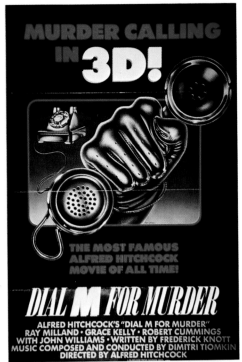

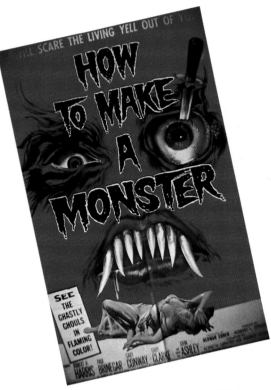

One-sheet poster for *How to Make a Monster* (1958). The movie was a bomb, but the poster was brilliant.

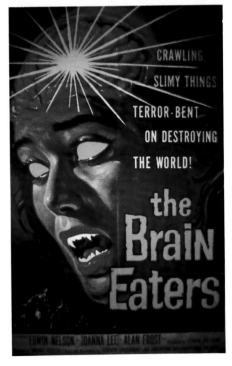

One-sheet poster from *The Brain Eaters* (1958).

# CHAPTER 2

# The Many Ways of Collecting Movie Memorabilia

**M**Y FIRST COLLECTION of movie-related material was a pile of "monster magazines" stored in a box in my closet. I was 10 years old, and while I didn't realize it at the time, movies had already spun their special sort of magic all around me, in the toys and games received on holidays, in the music my parents played on the hi-fi, in the television programs I watched, and in the comics I read.

Like most baby boomers in America, as a kid I wore Mickey Mouse pajamas and Superman socks. I had a Hopalong Cassidy six-shooter and a Roy Rogers cowboy hat. I saw *Pinocchio* and *The Wizard of Oz* at the theater. But it was that modest pile of monster magazines that represented my first conscious effort to collect movie material, bizarre as it was.

Those cheaply printed publications contained dozens of publicity photos of classic film monsters, like the Mummy and Quasimodo. They contained retrospective articles about silent films such as *Nosferatu* and *The Lost World*. They contained teaser announcements of films currently under production in Hollywood, like *The Seventh Voyage of Sinbad* (1958) and *The House on Haunted Hill* (1958).

The magazines provided everything a 10-year-old boy could wish for—well, almost everything. Any conceivable omissions were made up for in the offers in the back of the magazines. Most magazines had several pages of ads offering additional items to collect: makeup kits and lagoon monster masks, the novels that inspired *The Village of the Damned* (1960) and *Donovan's Brain* (1953), long-playing record albums featuring themes from horror movies, and the most exciting items of all—actual film strips from *The Bride of Frankenstein* (1935) and *It Came from Outer Space* (1953), plus a battery-operated 8mm home-movie projector that goes anywhere and projects scenes from, say, *The Phantom of the Opera* (1925), on "any clear surface!" My seemingly insignificant stack of monster magazines was in reality a doorway into the Hollywood dream factory, and I—like millions of other kids—was eager to possess a part, if not all, of the dream.

**Fig. 2-1.** Publication cel from D.C. Heath Book Series of Mickey Mouse and nephew, gouache on celluloid; 7″ × 8″. This cel is not from a cartoon, but it is authentic Disney. (© Walt Disney Corp.)

**Fig. 2-2.** Lobby card headlining Fred Astaire and Ginger Rogers in *Shall We Dance* (1937).

Fig. 2-3. Part of the strange magazine ad campaign for *Sirocco* (1951) featuring an equally strange trench-coated Humphrey Bogart in the desert.

Yes, I'd been bitten hard by the movie collecting bug. My first collection of movie memorabilia had all of the basic elements that make collecting so much fun. It had an association with powerful emotional events: I loved and hated those movie monsters. I had a feeling of uniqueness: I alone owned this particular collection of "valuable and rare treasures." And it had a way of vividly connecting me to another place and time (even if I'd never seen a particular original motion picture): I could imagine clearly what it would be like to stand on the moon, or in an ancient castle, or in a Hollywood production studio.

When you look at a piece of Hollywood history, it stirs the memories of the first time you experienced a particular film or viewed a performer's art. These vague feelings

**Fig. 2-4.** Rita Hayworth ad for Lux soap. In the 1940s, Hollywood stars were often employed to promote products. According to the ad, Rita is not alone, since "9 out of 10 screen stars use Lux."

and yearnings are "the stuff that dreams are made of," and they are part of the magic spell that movie memorabilia weaves over its collectors. Almost any collector of movie material starts with these same exciting feelings and then gradually ends up as one of a variety of collector types, depending on what interests are developed.

Collectors can be divided into three major types. The first type is interested exclusively in original items and concerned with building a collection for personal satisfaction and edification, without any thought as to the uses to which such a collection might be

Fig. 2-5. Classic movie still of James Coburn and Rod Steiger from *Duck, You Sucker* (1971).

put. This type of collector—call him or her a Film Fan—wants a color still photograph from *Gone With the Wind* because it's a "must have" item valued for individual personal enjoyment.

The second type of collector is enthusiastic about the scholarly aspects of motion pictures. This collector—an Archivist Collector—might be employed by a museum or movie studio and will likely want to acquire the same still the Film Fan is after but will want it for use with a proposed article or book to be presented publicly. This type of collector studies film technique and history with the intent to teach or contribute to it.

The third type of collector isn't really a collector at all, but rather a Dealer. Typically, a Dealer is very interested in and knowledgeable about film material but has decided to

**Fig. 2-6.** Stylish window card of Shirley Temple in her first star vehicle *Bright Eyes* (1934); 22″ × 28″. Heavy card stock, stiff enough to stand up in a store window, was used for these kinds of cards.

let the majority of available movie items pass through to other buyers while accepting a profit for the transfer. Dealers operate stores, manufacture collecting supplies, run tables at conventions, and seek out movie memorabilia primarily for investment value. The vast majority of movie material available to you today is the result of the diligent efforts of Dealers.

Value and collectibility has little to do with age of an item as far as movie memorabilia is concerned. For example, there is little interest in collecting one-of-a-kind pieces of film-projecting equipment from the early 1900s, but there is a cult following for anything connected with Marilyn Monroe, James Dean, Humphrey Bogart, or Judy Garland. Thus, what is rare is not always what is greatly valued by collectors. ''Star quality'' is the dominant factor affecting the value of a specific piece of film memorabilia, be it a unique item or a mass-produced product.

There are three types of movie memorabilia: the unique item, the mass-produced film promotional item, and the mass-produced licensed item.

Examples of unique items are the costume worn by Tyrone Power in *The Mark of Zorro,* the Superman costume worn by George Reeves in the television series (see color section), and the original mat painting of an alien landscape from *Forbidden Planet.* Examples of mass-produced film promotional items include a 41″ × 27″ poster promoting the 1956 production *Giant* (featuring Elizabeth Taylor, Rock Hudson, and James Dean) and a souvenir program for *The Birth of a Nation.* Examples of mass-produced licensed items include *Star Wars* action figure dolls and Popeye dime banks.

Many people assemble collections related to a specific actor or director; that is, they might want memorabilia associated with John Wayne or Erich von Stroheim. This approach is particularly appealing to the collector who enjoys the art of movies as much as the individual stories they tell. It allows the collector to see how an artist has developed skills and trends over the years and exposes the collector to a variety of characters and concepts that the performer or director has handled.

A few collectors try to collect all of the movie items produced by a particular company, for example, Disney material or Republic westerns. However, company identity meant a lot more back in the 1930s and 1940s than it does today, and it doesn't seem

**Fig. 2-8.** Film version of hardback Dashiell Hammett novel *The Glass Key* (1942). The dustjacket displays stars Brian Donlevy, Veronica Lake, and Alan Ladd.

right to miss out on material you'd like to collect just because it doesn't have the right studio name on it.

One collector I know makes a point of collecting at least one item from every movie ever made. This collecting approach can be a lot of fun but it also can be very expensive. Furthermore, while the idea is a noble one—if you choose to pursue this course it will expose you to the entire industry—it can also fill your collection with a lot of memorabilia that isn't very memorable.

Another way of collecting is to gather together material of a certain film type, or

**Fig. 2-9.** *Screen Hits Annual #8* (1953). Cover photos of Debbie Reynolds, Liz Taylor, and John Wayne make this magazine a premium find.

genre. You might want to collect items associated with James Bond films, or Andy Hardy films, or Sherlock Holmes films, or musicals, or mysteries, or science fiction films. One person I know is a fan of Japanese monster movies and has lobby cards, posters, models, and videos of films like *Godzilla* and *Mothra*.

Finally, some collectors specialize in movies of a certain time period or style. For example, you might like film noir or movies made during World War II, because of their general tone or content. This sort of collecting can include any subclass or any combination of categories, such as horror cowboy flicks (*Jesse James Meets Frankenstein's Daughter*) or pseudo-documentaries (*Glen or Glenda*).

What's the best way to collect movie memorabilia? Easy—collect the stuff that appeals to you. Look at lots of films and then decide which ones are your top 10 favorites. Try to find a pattern to your interests. Are comedies what you enjoy most? Or does your

**Fig. 2-10.** An autographed and inscribed photo of Barbara Billingsley, best known for her role in the "Leave It to Beaver" television show.

taste run more to historical epics, like *Ben-Hur* and *Glory*? Do you like B movies and serials? The film category that appeals to you most should guide your collecting because that's the sort of movie you'd like to see remembered in the future. And what else is memorabilia for, if not to celebrate the memory of something you like?

In the long run, *collect what you like* is probably the single most important piece of advice you'll find in this book. The popularity of a specific movie is often only a fad. Today's big box-office hit will soon be replaced by another winner, so it's not a good idea to buy movie memorabilia expecting that someday it will make you rich, because it may never happen. However, if you collect what you like, you'll have hours of enjoyment regardless of fluctuating prices and the whims of popular taste. It's your collection, right? Why not collect what you want, instead of following the crowd, the big parade, or the lost patrol?

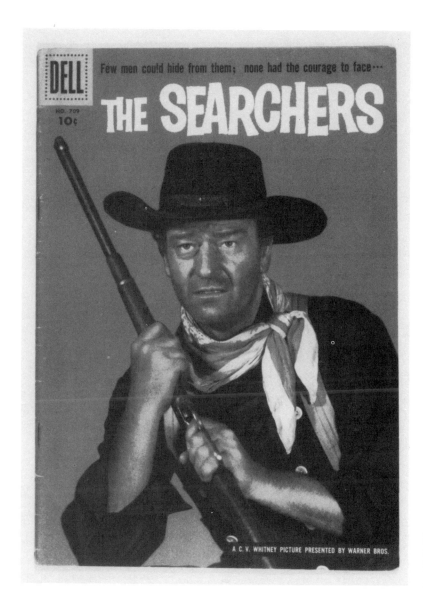

**Fig. 2-11.** Dell Comics adaptation of the John Ford/John Wayne film *The Searchers* (1956).

# CHAPTER 3

# How to Get Started

**W**HEN I BEGAN TO COLLECT movie memorabilia seriously, I felt I was at a disadvantage because my home in Ohio was so far removed from the Hollywood dream factory. I had forgotten, at first, that Hollywood had spent decades trying to reach my home and the homes of millions of others like me. Over the years, they'd sent thousands of films to local theaters, along with literally tons of promotional material: posters and lobby cards for the theaters, press releases with photos, movie ads for the newspapers, as well as hours of air time on radio and television stations and row after row of magazines at the newsstands.

The effects of Hollywood and the movies were already documented in dozens of books and on microfilm at my local library. The nearby university had several original scripts in its Rare Book Room. The television stations in my area presented old movies every morning, afternoon, evening, and night. But none of this seemed to satisfy the yearning I felt to be personally connected to my favorite star or movie.

I began collecting more seriously by picking my favorite films (*Goldfinger* and *The Road to Hong Kong*) and diligently searching all available media for information that would allow me to extend the exciting feeling I'd experienced while watching those movies up on the silver screen. I bought the soundtrack album, read and clipped newspaper reports, and purchased magazines that contained feature articles or photographs from the movies. Like many other fans, I went back to the theater to see a favorite movie again and again. At the theater, I often asked for a program book or inquired if I could possibly buy the poster after the theater was finished with it.

It seemed as if I were assembling a mysterious jigsaw puzzle or maintaining a sacred trust by seeking out this information and preserving it for future study. No doubt about it, Hollywood had reached out and made contact with me; I was a teenage film fan.

All of us, to some extent, have been contacted by Hollywood. And just about everyone owns at least one prized item of movie memorabilia that he or she would think twice about before selling. Perhaps it's a well-worn record, or an autographed photo, or an old issue of *Modern Screen,* or a videotape of *Bladerunner.* In many cases it is a casual or happenstance ownership—an impulse buy or a lucky find. But if you want to expand your collection, you need to find experienced sources of information that will tell you where to find more and better movie memorabilia.

Where can you find such a friend? How can you safely get started collecting in this strange and busy world of movie memorabilia? Beyond this book, I can think of six other places to go to get good advice and learn more about movie material: other collectors, the library, local movie collectibles shops, film conventions, collector publications, and auctions.

# Other Collectors

It probably doesn't seem likely to you that there are other collectors of movie memorabilia in your immediate area, but don't underestimate the power of Hollywood to reach out and cultivate its public. Within every major city there is an arts museum, a college, a theater group, or a movie house that specializes in reviving old movies. Each of these places is an avenue for discovering people who share your interests. Many of these institutions hold regularly scheduled meetings to view and discuss films. Or you could meet another collector by chance at any time, and once you've met one, there's always another that that person knows, and another, and another, and another.

Also, don't forget to tell your friends and relatives of your interest. In many cases, older relatives have long ago been bitten by the movie memorabilia bug and have boxes full of movie magazines and other mementos they will share with you or even turn over to you (if you catch them in a fit of spring cleaning). Their collecting knowledge can greatly expand yours as they tell you about the cherished items they have saved.

# The Library

The public library is a wonderful place to read up on your favorite hobby. There you're sure to find lots of books and back-issue magazines on films and Hollywood. Oftentimes, an interlibrary loan will net you even more material. And don't forget the videos you can borrow and the microfilm files where you can learn still more about your favorite motion-picture topics.

# The Local Movie Collectibles Shop

If you search the Yellow Pages in your area under "Collectibles" and "Antiques," you will be amazed at how many sources for movie memorabilia are within only a few miles of your home. In many instances, you'll find that there is a store near you that specializes in the sale of old movie material as well as other popular-culture items such as comic books and sport cards.

**Fig. 3-1.** Collecting film at a film convention.

A beginning collector can get a good education in collecting movie memorabilia just by spending a few hours in one of these stores. There you'll be able to meet other collectors and get a feel for a host of movie items you never knew existed. You'll get a chance to talk with people who share your interest, enabling you to ask questions and get lots of valuable information while making new friends.

Most important, you'll be able to buy, trade, and maybe even sell movie material at a specialty shop, as well as pick up supplies for your hobby such as storage boxes and poster frames.

# Film Conventions

A movie convention is the absolute best place to learn about your hobby, but you've got to be alert. There's lots going on at a movie convention, and it's almost too much to take in.

At a movie convention you will see thousands of old and rare movie items available for sale or trade. You'll meet other film fans and collectors who share your interests.

**Fig. 3-2.** Collecting photos at a film convention.

**Fig. 3-3.** Viewing films at a film convention.

**Fig. 3-4.** The three specialty newspapers that support the collecting of movie memorabilia: *Big Reel, Movie Collector's World,* and *Classic Images.*

Sometimes, you'll even get to talk to famous guest stars who are appearing at the convention, people who were part of Hollywood during its golden age. You might win a door prize, get an autograph, and listen to a panel discussion about the future of the industry. And you can watch lots of rare or "lost" films from private collections (see Fig. 3-3).

Movie conventions are held all over the country. Major shows occur each year in New York, Atlanta, Columbus, Knoxville, Memphis, and Hollywood. Finding out about conventions is easy. Just ask the operators of your local collectibles shop or check the listings in the movie collector publications. (See the Resources section of this book for the addresses of major conventions.)

# Collector Publications

The best way to understand what's happening in the movie memorabilia world is to read regularly several of the monthly newspapers that focus on collecting film material. These publications can be purchased at your antiques or collectibles shop or subscribed to by

TWENTY COMPLETE STORIES FOR FIVE CENTS

# Hollywood

HOLLYWOOD
5¢

DECEMBER

CLARK GABLE

## WHY GABLE IS TODAY'S TOPIC FOR GOSSIP

**Fig. 3-5.** *Hollywood* magazine with stunning cover photo of Clark Gable, December 1941.

mail. They usually feature news, letter columns, articles, ads, and important listings of upcoming conventions. From these publications, you can develop a feel for the marketplace and a sense of history for your hobby. The three main publications you'll want to look for are *Classic Images,* P.O. Box 809, Muscatine, Iowa 52761; *Movie Collector's World,* P.O. Box 309, Fraser, MI 48026; and *The Big Reel,* Empire Publishing, Route #3, Box 83, Madison, NC 27025 (see Fig. 3-4).

# Auctions

One of the most exciting ways to learn about one-of-a-kind movie memorabilia is through an auction. Several times each year, major auction houses publish catalogs detailing

**Fig. 3-6.** Cheesecake—autographed still of Brigit Bardot; 8″ × 11″.

hundreds of items placed on sale to the public. These catalogs usually describe each item and include a photograph and tell you a host of inside information about the popular movie or Hollywood personality with which the item is associated.

Naturally, you can bid on any item described in the catalog to give yourself the chance of owning it. Auctions can help you learn about your hobby while picking up a bargain from the comfort of your own home.

Major sources for movie memorabilia auctions are:

■ Camden House, 10921 Wilshire Blvd., Suite 808, Los Angeles, CA 90024
■ Hake's Americana & Collectibles, P.O. Box 1444, York, PA 17405
■ Christie's East, 219 E. 67th St., New York, NY 10021
■ Sotheby's, 1334 York Ave., New York, NY 10021

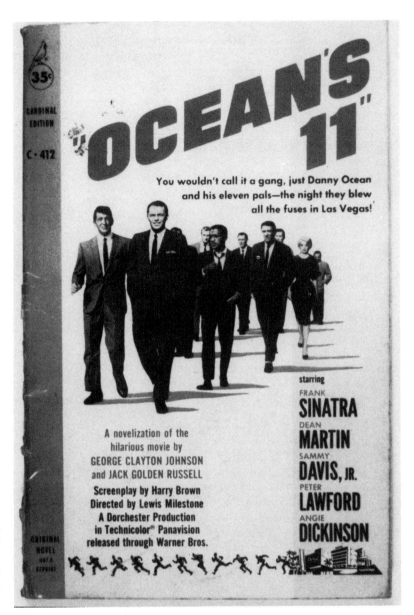

**Fig. 3-7.** Paperback novelization of *Ocean's 11* (1960). The book's ending to the story is much more depressing than that presented in the film.

Fig. 3-8. Special reorchestrated and recomposed film score from *Torn Curtain* (1966). This is not the original soundtrack; this album is conducted by Elmer Bernstein rather than the original composer, Bernard Herrmann.

Fig. 3-9. Half-sheet poster of *Spider Woman* (1943), a World War II Sherlock Holmes adventure; 22″ × 28″.

**Fig. 3-10.** Glossy publicity/production still of Alfred Hitchcock and Tippi Hedren.

A mail-order auction is easy, exciting and fun. If you bid and win an item of movie memorabilia, you can expect to pay for shipping and handling charges to get it to you in addition to the bid price. But from that point on—it's yours!

Since there's such a wealth of information available to even the beginning collector, there's no better time to start collecting than right now. All you need to know is a little inside information about the major collecting categories and an idea of their basic values. The next seven chapters will give you details about collecting over 15 different types of movie memorabilia. Let's go!

Fig. 3-11. One-sheet poster of alluring Bette Davis from *Now, Voyager* (1946); 41″ × 27″.

# CHAPTER 4

# Posters, Lobby Cards, and Stills

I ONCE HELD IN MY HANDS over half a million dollars in movie memorabilia and let it slip through my fingers for lack of $300. It was the early seventies, and I had a couple dozen movie posters and lobby card sets and a stack of stills from *Gone With the Wind* and *The Wizard of Oz* all piled up and ready for purchase. Then I decided to let them go; it seemed like a frivolous purchase, at the time. I told myself that this was all just a bunch of old paper used to promote 30-year-old movies, and $300 was, well, $300. But had I gone ahead and bought these items, I'd probably be independently wealthy today. Probably.

I know now that I'd been lucky to find these items and unlucky to have decided not to buy them. The lesson I learned was that you've got to be quick and smart to get the good stuff—and the whole purpose of this book is to keep you from making a similar mistake.

The three most popular types of movie memorabilia are the poster, the lobby card, and the still photograph. Until the recent advent of videotape, these "frozen" visuals were the most common ways for average people to own pieces of their favorite films.

## Movie Posters

The most popular movie collectible is the poster. No longer found exclusively in theater lobbies, movie posters have made the scene in restaurants, museums, art galleries, and living rooms across the nation. In addition, the general public has begun to understand that movie posters are a cheap and safe form of art investment.

Posters promoting individual films did not come into use in the United States until 1909, when exhibitors began to demand visually interesting materials to promote their visually interesting movies. Thus, movie studios began toying with color posters around

Fig. 4-1. Colorful one-sheet poster depicting straight-shooter Tom Mix in early talkie serial *The Miracle Rider* (1935).

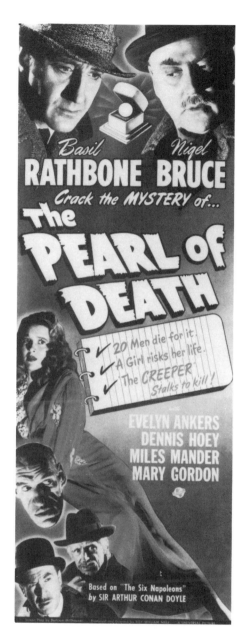

Fig. 4-2. Insert poster for *The Pearl of Death* (1944) featuring Basil Rathbone, Nigel Bruce, and the Creeper; 36" × 14".

Fig. 4-3. Title card from a set of lobby cards for *The Navigator* (1924). Buster Keaton firmly established himself as a Chaplin contender in this gag-filled and often-thrilling comedy set on a schooner at sea.

Fig. 4-4. Half-sheet poster for *Terror by Night* (1946); a fine graphic representation of Sherlock Holmes mystery/adventure.

**Fig. 4-5.** Title lobby card for *The Oklahoma Kid* (1939), starring James Cagney and Humphrey Bogart.

**Fig. 4-6.** Unusual and over-sized lobby card of *Anna Christie* (1930), Garbo's first talkie; 14″ × 17″.

the time of World War I, mixing traditional concepts in oil painting with then-popular trends in billboard advertising.

The earliest printed posters promoting movies are interesting to collectors of the history of cinema, advertising, or printing, but they have very little appeal or value to most collectors of movie memorabilia. The chief reason is that the early printed "hand-bills," with their simple lists of film titles, portrayed little if anything of the visual excitement of the moving-picture medium.

After World War I, the country entered a boom period that witnessed the rise of opulent movie palaces. These grand entertainment centers presented the public with ceiling murals, chandeliers, royal viewing boxes, and, significant for movie poster evolution, attractive streetfront entrances featuring display cases for maximum exposure of movie graphics.

During the 1920s and 1930s, many large first-run theaters used their own handprinted posters and often created elaborate displays for major film productions. It was not until later in the 1930s that offset lithograph printing came into use, and though images were clearer, posters lacked the rich color and texture found in the earlier stone lithography.

During this era, movie studios distributed their own posters. Each company had an individual style; for example, the subtle delicacy of RKO Radio Pictures with its pastel and watercolor images contrasted with the clear, uncluttered look of MGM's bright primary colors.

All this beauty notwithstanding, movie posters were meant to sell movies and not to be sold themselves. Consequently, thousands and thousands of gorgeous and glamorous posters were thrown out for lack of interest or storage space after a film had come and gone. In fact, many posters from the 1920s and 1930s were donated to the paper drives of World War II.

After the war, the artistry in movie posters declined; studios, under pressure from the rising star of television, cut costs. The posters of the 1950s and 1960s, with only a few exceptions, were often no more than pasteups from tinted photos and flat lettering. But by the end of the 1970s, the usefulness of a visually grabbing movie poster came back as big box-office films like *Star Wars, E.T.*, and the *Indiana Jones* series brought a spirit of youthful fun back into the theaters.

There are four basic types of collectible movie posters that are very popular among collectors: the one-sheet, the half-sheet, the insert, and the window card. All are of slightly different dimensions and are used for slightly different purposes.

In addition to these four basic sizes, several larger movie posters were made available in the 1930s, 1940s, and early 1950s (see Fig. 4-12). These include the three-sheet, which is three times the size of a one-sheet; the six-sheet, which is six times the size of the one-sheet; and the twenty-four-sheet billboard poster, which is twenty-four times the size of a one-sheet and almost impossible to collect, let alone display. Collector interest in these larger posters is less than for the four basic types, so the value of the larger posters is often less than that of the basic posters, rather than more.

The one-sheet poster (27" × 41") would often be produced in two versions or styles for a given movie. Both styles are usually worth the same price, but in some cases one style might be more graphically desirable among collectors (and thus more valuable) because it features a better design or more dramatic images of star players.

The half-sheet poster (22″ × 28″) is roughly half the size of a one-sheet and is wider than it is tall. During the 1930s, the half-sheets from MGM and RKO were just as pretty as the one-sheets, but in later years this form was slighted artistically in favor of the more standard posters. In many cases, half-sheets were no more than larger versions of the same art presented on the title card (see "Lobby Cards," in this chapter).

The insert poster (14″ × 36″) is also roughly half the size of a one-sheet, and it is taller than it is wide. Because of its unusual vertical format, good insert art was often a challenge to produce, and the results are often appealing.

The window card poster (14″ × 22″) is printed on heavier card stock than most one-sheet posters so that it will stand up in a window. These cards were distributed around town by local theater owners to be placed in the front windows of drugstores, barbershops, and newsstands. The upper portion of the card was left blank so that the theater owner could add play dates and theater names to the movie graphics. In many instances, this local information has been cut away, leaving a poster card 14″ × 18″ in size.

## Movie Poster Values

A small difference in price exists between a poster in average condition and one in excellent condition. Not enough difference in value exists to set up a separate price for average condition and excellent condition. A sliding scale is used to determine values of most movie posters (and, for that matter, the values of most other types of movie memorabilia as well). A certain amount of damage (thumbtack holes or minor tape marks from when the poster hung in a theater display case) is acceptable. Also, keep in mind that posters were almost always folded, and therefore creases are expected and acceptable.

Condition, beauty of graphics, and stars featured are the three factors that play an important role in determining the value of any movie poster.

Until recently, you couldn't really own a copy of a film on videotape or videodisc. Since film is a visual and somewhat intangible art form, there was only one alternative for the film lover—collecting that which was tangible and accessible and which captured the mood and style of the film, as well as displaying its stars. Thus, people who wanted to possess the spirit of a movie collected movie posters.

Many collectors believe that with the advent of videotape and videodisc the demand for movie posters will decline. I don't agree. Rather, it seems to me that the increased interest in films due to the popularity of video will translate into an increased interest in printed movie memorabilia. In addition, the printed movie material will now be viewed with respect for itself, instead of being seen as a substitute for the film. Thus, demand will probably increase and prices of printed movie material will go up.

Supply and demand—along with what collectors can or are willing to pay—establish a poster's worth today. Boosts to poster value include the death of a performer or media

**Fig. 4-7.** Window card for the last great Mae West film, *Klondike Annie* (1936). Note the imprint at the top of the card describing the date and theater of the film's showing.

focus on the performer for some reason; stage, screen, or television appearances by a performer; and any new version or remake of an old film. Such occurrences catch public attention and increase the demand for the poster, which in turn increases the price.

Pieces of classic movie memorabilia still receive classic prices. Significant posters from original American releases include those from *The Thief of Bagdad* (1924), *The Phantom of the Opera* (1925), *King Kong* (1933), *The Adventures of Robin Hood* (1938), *Gone With the Wind* (1939), *The Wizard of Oz* (1939), *Citizen Kane* (1941), *The Maltese Falcon* (1941), and *Casablanca* (1942). However, posters for popular films released in the last 10 years are typically available for as little as $5.

The popularity of many classic films caused the studios to re-release them after a decade or so to a new generation of moviegoers. In doing this, the studios often re-

Fig. 4-8. One-sheet poster for *Niagara* (1953), highly prized due to dramatic art of Marilyn Monroe.

released the classic posters, too, or commissioned an entirely new poster campaign for a re-released film. While many reissue posters have better graphics than the originals, re-release poster values are a fraction of the value of the original poster.

In the greatest number of cases, you can tell if a poster is an original or a re-release by studying the date code number usually found in the poster's lower right corner. If the poster has a number beginning with the letter *R*, as in R54/197, you know that you have

**Fig. 4-9.** Three big name stars on one window card advertising the MGM bonanza *The Last of Mrs. Cheyney* (1937).

before you a re-release version of the poster. In this example, the number 54 signifies the year that the film was re-released, and the number 197 signifies that this poster (an insert for the 1934 movie *The Lost Patrol*) is the 197th item issued in 1954.

If there is no number and no sign of tampering with that area of the poster, you're probably looking at an original. Take time to look on the poster for telltale words like ''re-release'' or ''encore-presentation,'' sure signs that the poster is not from the film's original run.

Occasionally, you will find a poster of a movie with the correct original release date code, but superimposed on the artwork will be a little picture of an Oscar and writing indicating the film was an Academy Award winner. This poster is called an ''Oscar'' or an ''Award'' poster and is not considered original issue.

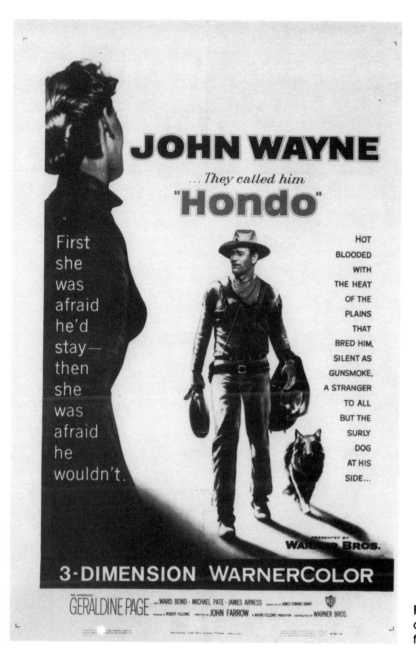

**Fig. 4-10.** One-sheet poster of 3-D John Wayne feature film *Hondo* (1955).

**Fig. 4-11.** One-sheet poster from *Leave Her To Heaven* (1946), a beautiful technicolor film noir. Gene Tierney is equally beautiful.

**Fig. 4-12.** Oversized linen-backed poster from *Singin' in the Rain* (1952); 81″ × 41″.

**Fig. 4-13.** Marilyn seductively beckons in this collectible poster from *Bus Stop* (1956), one of her best performances.

One of the best ways to tell the difference between old and new posters is to feel the paper. Slick paper wasn't used in posters in the early years, so a poster for *Dracula* (1930) that brightly reflects the light is probably a reprint. Also, you can check the original press book, if it is available to you, to see if a poster appears there in illustration; this approach can provide reliable information about an old poster's design and availability.

For the average collector, re-release posters mean the collector can enjoy substantial savings over expensive originals while at the same time collecting items that still have value in terms of both graphics and investment potential. For example, the posters of the 1949 re-release of *The Wizard of Oz* look almost the same as the original 1939 release posters but sell for a fraction of the price of original posters.

Classic American films were also released overseas, so there are also foreign versions of American movie posters. Usually the title and the cast names are in English, but the rest of the poster's information is in another language. Values for such items are wide open because some collectors want anything beautiful associated with a film or movie star, while other collectors are put off by the strangeness of the foreign language.

If you discover an old one-sheet that has never been folded and shows little wear or a poster that falls outside the various dimensions mentioned earlier, be very suspicious because the piece may be a commercial reproduction. Most reproductions are legitimate; that is, they are done with no intent to fool you. Usually, legitimate reproductions have the copyright date of the company doing the reproduction in the poster's border. However, if you don't see a name printed along the poster's edge but you detect flaws from the original poster (such as pin holes or fold marks) reproduced in the new photo offset copy, then you know that you are looking at a reproduction.

Due to the growth of popularity of movie posters among collectors during the past years, many dealers and collectors have gotten retired actors and actresses, as well as producers and directors, to autograph posters for movies made 30 or more years ago. The recent autographs on such posters may enhance their value somewhat, but not all collectors think that new autographs add to the charm of an original poster. (See Chapter 10 for more information on the subject of autographs.)

# Lobby Cards

As noted in the previous sections, movie posters generally display original artwork and sometimes sport photographs and abstract graphics as well. On the other hand, lobby cards almost always are limited to showing a series of photographs from the actual movie. Lobby cards are 11″ × 14″ and, except for some re-release material and serials, almost always come in sets of eight. (A printer can produce eight cards from a sheet of paper the size of a one-sheet movie poster.)

Lobby cards are usually printed on heavier, more durable paper stock than posters are and are numbered. Card number one is called the title card. The title card often contains a small version of the artwork that is on the promotional poster. The major characters from the film are almost always on the title card. The other seven cards, called scene cards, do not usually depict a major actor but instead show minor figures or simply a scene from the movie. Alone, a title card is almost always worth more than any one other card in the set. In fact, some collectors specialize in title cards.

Some movies have great lobby sets and some do not. When buying sets of cards, it is wise to make sure that the title card is included and to see if many of the other seven cards depict major stars. Title cards rival one-sheets as the number-one poster collectible for many reasons. They are easy to transport and display in picture book albums, and they don't require folding and unfolding, as posters do. Plus, title cards can be used to make a very attractive display in a very small space.

As the name suggests, lobby cards were produced for display in theater lobbies to announce coming attractions or to heighten anticipation for the current feature. The earliest known lobby cards were produced by Universal in sets of four. Unlike later cards, some of these early ones were intended for vertical as well as horizontal display. The first cards were in shades of black or brown and white, and it was not until around 1917 that full-color cards began to appear. By the early 1920s all lobby cards were in full color, with the exception of those produced to promote short subjects and serials.

In addition to regular lobby cards, some studios offered still photographs in the form of lobby cards, complete with a title card and the advertising matter below each scene. This practice enabled the theater to get double-duty from lobby cards and photographs for newspaper publicity.

The value of lobby cards, like any type of movie memorabilia, is governed by the celebrity or film they depict. The highest price paid for a single lobby card is believed to be $5,000 for a title card from *The Wizard of Oz*. Lobby cards depicting principal characters in any of the following films generally sell for around $1,000 each: *Casablanca, Gone With the Wind, The Wizard of Oz, The Maltese Falcon, King Kong*.

Lobby cards from the silent era vary tremendously in price, due to the random and fading interest in silent film stars. But a title card from *The Navigator* (1924) starring Buster Keaton recently sold at a Camden House auction for over $3,000 (see Fig. 4-3).

Reproductions of lobby cards have come into vogue of late. For only a few dollars, you can buy photographic reproductions of classic lobbies that, in their original form, would cost hundreds, sometimes thousands of dollars. Thus, you can still acquire a beautiful reprint of your favorite movie scene at an affordable price.

# Stills

Still photographs are posed pictures, usually 8″ × 10″, taken on the movie set during or immediately before (or after) filming. Stills are typically of a specific scene from a film, but they may also be candid, showing the production staff at work or the players relaxing prior to a take, perhaps reading a script. Portrait or publicity photos are usually retouched to present stars in their best light, while candid shots are more natural.

Most stills from Hollywood's golden era are black-and-white. Occasionally, these will have been tinted for dramatic effect. Of course, more recent movies have color stills. The backs of older stills often have the stamps of the studios or photographers who were associated with them and even the date.

**Fig. 4-14.** Glossy black-and-white still of Bette Davis and Leslie Howard from *The Petrified Forest* (1936).

Like lobby cards, stills are easy to store and display in a ring binder or on the wall. They are the item most easily traded with other collectors. Prices for stills increase slowly, unlike those of other movie memorabilia, so that it is possible to build an important, very selective collection of originals that will be every bit as unforgettable, entertaining, and fresh as the movies they represent—while they increase steadily in value.

Starting a collection of stills with a general interest in mind offers many advantages, chief of which is being able to see, feel, and experiment with the immense variety of stills of a more specialized character. The kinds of stills that are in the greatest demand feature one or more of the following:

- Comedy teams like the Marx Brothers and Laurel and Hardy
- Horror films like *Dracula* and *Aliens*

**Fig. 4-15.** Frame blowup still of Errol Flynn as Robin Hood. The hazy quality is typical of stills made from enlarging a frame of movie film.

- Mystery movies like those of Charlie Chan and Sherlock Holmes
- Westerns and Western stars
- Serials and cliffhangers
- Big-name stars like Bogart, Garbo, Elvis, and Marilyn
- Directors like Hitchcock, Ford, and Lucas
- Musicals like *Singin' in the Rain* and *Hair*
- Sexy stars like Rita Hayworth and Ann Margret
- Teen idols like Michael J. Fox and Molly Ringwald

Like stamps in a philatelist's collection, stills can be grouped into unique and interesting specializations. I've seen still collections of stunts, close-ups, Academy Awards,

**Fig. 4-16.** Classic publicity still of Douglas Fairbanks and Billie Dove from *The Black Pirate* (1926).

and animation. Almost any aspect of film that attracts you can be recorded in a specialized collection of stills.

Originally, the purpose of stills was to appear in local newspapers and magazines to attract attention for films and stars. This created the cheesecake and the beefcake images associated with Hollywood performers. The main value of these kinds of photographs is that they provide a record of a performer at a particular moment in his or her career. The age of a still is not always a good indication of its value.

"ROPE"
Directed by ALFRED HITCHCOCK
A UNIVERSAL CLASSIC

Director **ALFRED HITCHCOCK** rehearses his cast as the
various technicians look on.

5315-5

**Fig. 4-17.** Behind-the-scenes photo from Alfred Hitchcock's *Rope* (1948).

For original photos of first-release movies, the surface finish of a still is nearly always very glossy. Stills from the late 1920s and early 1930s are in a semigloss and sometimes matte or textured finish. Before 1925, all stills were made with a dull finish, and the color was often the brownish tint (sepia) popular at that time. A high-gloss still depicting a film made before 1925 is probably a recent copy of an old photo.

Even the best-preserved glossy stills will show minor cracks in their finish after half a century. In time, slow drying of the photographic film itself will cause crackling in the gloss surface. Recent copies of original stills, or "dupes," will not show these effects of aging. Such copies are attractive but are not as valuable as originals.

Available in addition to the types of stills described above are frame enlargments, that is, photos enlarged directly from frames of film stock. These stills are often used by scholars or historians to illustrate a point exactly as it appears in a film. Such frame enlargements are generally grainy or blurred and are therefore shunned by collectors looking for glamour and photographic quality (see Fig. 4-15).

**Fig. 4-18.** Candid still of James Cagney and Boris Karloff.

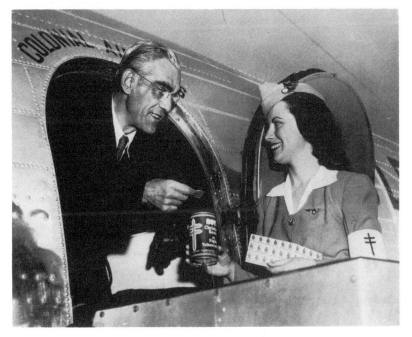

**Fig. 4-19.** Publicity still of Boris Karloff helping to promote Christmas Seals.

**Fig. 4-20.** Portrait still of Boris Karloff.

"FRANKENSTEIN" *a Universal Picture* MADE IN U.S.A.

Collections of color photographs, negatives, and antique glass slides are popular. All of these forms of photographic movie memorabilia can help collectors tap into the warmth and entertainment of the original film.

Millions of attractive photos are available for only a few dollars from dozens of mail-order houses and movie memorabilia shops throughout the country. Even a fledgling collector can afford a terrific display of stills and then move on to the larger, more colorful, and more valuable posters and lobby cards. Assembling a specialized collection of such memorabilia is one of the best ways to commemorate your favorite Hollywood personality or production.

**Fig. 4-21.** Production still of Boris Karloff from *The Body Snatcher* (1945).

# Example Prices

There are price guides available for you to use for reference as you buy and sell your movie memorabilia. While this book is not a price guide, it seems helpful here to list a few current 1991 prices for various items, just to give you an idea of the wide range of prices involved—and to show that there is something out there for just about any budget. Below are some sample prices for items in mint condition:

## Posters

**One-sheets**

| | |
|---|---|
| *Sherlock Holmes Pursuit to Algiers* (1945) | $850 |
| *Secret Service in Darkest Africa* (1943) | 125 |
| *Adventures of the Red Ryder* (1940) | 285 |
| *Madame X* (1937) | 250 |
| *Tarzan and the Leopard Woman* (1946) | 450 |
| *As Young As You Feel* (1951), M. Monroe | 150 |
| *For Me and My Gal* (1942), J. Garland | 575 |
| *Cat People* (1982) | 25 |
| *Cobs and Robbers* (1951), MGM cartoon | 150 |

### Three-sheets

| | |
|---|---|
| *Madame X* (1937) | $300 |
| *Jesse James at Bay* (1941), R. Rogers | 200 |
| *From Russia With Love* (1964), J. Bond | 175 |
| *Treasure of the Sierra Madre* (1948), H. Bogart | 2000 |

### Inserts

| | |
|---|---|
| *Red River* (1948), J. Wayne | $425 |
| *African Queen* (1951), H. Bogart | 450 |
| *Giant* (1956), J. Dean | 225 |
| *Tarzan's Secret Treasure* (1941) | 350 |
| *White Pants Willie* (1927) | 85 |
| *Rebecca* (1940), A. Hitchcock, 2 Oscars | 850 |
| *Madame X* (1937) | 125 |
| *Scared to Death* (1947), B. Lugosi | 75 |

### Half-sheets

| | |
|---|---|
| *Notorious* (1946), A. Hitchcock | $875 |
| *The Spoilers* (1930), G. Cooper | 650 |
| *Rain* (1932), J. Crawford | 450 |
| *The Big Sleep* (1946), H. Bogart | 325 |

# Window Cards

| | |
|---|---|
| *Forbidden Planet* (1956) | $450 |
| *China Seas* (1935), C. Gable, and J. Harlow | 950 |
| *Thunderball* (1965), J. Bond | 100 |
| *Fistful of Dollars* (1967), C. Eastwood | 95 |
| *Hound of the Baskervilles* (1939), B. Rathbone | 2500 |
| *Streetcar Named Desire* (1951), M. Brando | 125 |
| *Yankee Doodle Dandy* (1942), J. Cagney | 250 |

# Lobby Cards

### Lobby Card Sets

| | |
|---|---|
| *Tarzan and the Mermaids* (1948) | $150 |
| *In Harm's Way* (1965), J. Wayne | 50 |
| *The Invisible Boy* (1957), Robby the Robot | 150 |
| *I Was a Teenaged Frankenstein* (1957) | 100 |
| *Circus World* (1965), J. Wayne | 30 |
| *E.T.* (1982) | 25 |
| *Fahrenheit 451* (1967) | 30 |

## Lobby Title Cards

| | |
|---|---:|
| *On the Town* (1949), G. Kelly, F. Sinatra | $45 |
| *As Young As You Feel* (1951), M. Monroe | 95 |
| *Dinner at Eight* (1933), J. Harlow | 3500 |
| *Dr. Ehrlich's Magic Bullet,* (1940) E. Robinson | 200 |
| *So This Is Paris* (1926), E. Lubitsch | 850 |
| *Horror of Dracula* (1958) | 50 |
| *Mask of Dimitrios* (1944), P. Lorre, S. Greenstreet | 150 |
| *Yolonda* (1924) | 35 |

## Lobby "A" Cards

| | |
|---|---:|
| *Casablanca* (1942), H. Bogart | $350 |
| *Lifeboat* (1944) | 150 |
| *Santa Fe Trail* (1940), R. Reagan, E. Flynn | 200 |
| *Across the Pacific,* (1942), H. Bogart | 135 |
| *Swing Time* (1936), F. Astaire, G. Rogers | 200 |
| *Sands of Iwo Jima* (1949), J. Wayne | 45 |
| *Breakfast at Tiffany's* (1961) | 15 |
| *Gigi* (1958) | 10 |
| *Snow White and the Three Stooges* (1961) | 10 |

# Black-and-White Stills

| | |
|---|---:|
| *Bus Stop* (1956), M. Monroe | $150 |
| *Wizard of Oz* (1939) | 100 |
| Jean Harlow | 100 |
| Rita Hayworth | 250 |
| *Modern Times* (1936), C. Chaplin | 10 |
| Boris Karloff | 15 |
| Judy Garland | 400 |

# CHAPTER 5

# Books, Scripts, and Comics

**T**HERE IS A GREAT QUANTITY of printed readable movie memorabilia available to the movie enthusiast. From great tomes to read-at-a-sitting comics, the range offers something collectible for everyone.

I probably don't have to tell you that there are libraries and bookstores all over the map, stocked with shelves of movie and film books. Books in their various forms and formats are one of the easiest and least expensive ways to collect movie memorabilia.

I recently purchased a handsome volume that specialized in reviewing World War II films. It was particularly interesting because it focused only on movies that featured military aviation story lines. This meant that the film book (*When Hollywood Ruled the Skys,* by Bruce Orriss, Aero Associates, Inc., 1984) dealt in depth with only 47 movies, giving a new insight to this type of American film experience.

I also bought a nifty filmography (a biography of film appearances) about the actress Myrna Loy. Prior to purchasing this book, I was familiar with this beautiful, sometimes exotic-looking actress from her witty *Thin Man* series of films with William Powell and from her role in *The Best Years of Our Lives* (1946). But the book (*The Films of Myrna Loy,* by Lawrence Quirk, Citadel Press, 1980) described in great detail the more than 50 silent films Ms. Loy had appeared in and even more sound movies she had starred in well into the 1960s. I was impressed, amazed, and entertained.

And that is the value of film books. They share comprehensive and obscure information with you at affordable prices. I might never have known the connection between *A Yank in the R.A.F.* (1941) and *Hanover Street* (1979) without having read the book about World War II aviation films. In the same manner, I don't expect I'll ever see more than one-tenth of Myrna Loy's silent films, but the book I bought gave me a rich glimpse into these rare, forgotten, and lost silents.

Both books were bought at discount from a local bookstore. I paid $10 for the two and gained a wealth of movie entertainment to add to my collection for a very low price.

Among the best features of a collection of books about movies is its function as a readily available research library through which you can learn more about the movies and about movie collectibles. The variety of books available for purchase is about as great as the number of topics and types of films.

After a movie is over (and sometimes before), one of the best ways for a movie fan to capture the story of the film, sometimes in an expanded form, is through a special edition. That's why hundreds of "Photoplay Editions" were published by Grosset and Dunlap between 1913 and 1939. That's also why dozens of "novelizations" have been published every year since. Even the major film studios still get into the book business with commemorative program books. And, of course, hundreds of popular children's books and comics are published each year, all based on movie characters and themes, (for example, *The Indiana Jones Find-Your-Own Adventure Book,* the *Tarzan Pop-up Book,* and the comic book adaptation of *Dick Tracy*). This wealth of printed movie memorabilia also includes souvenir campaign books and even original scripts.

# Novelizations

For many people, the pleasures of a favorite movie are recalled by reading the story of the movie in a specially prepared book, often illustrated with choice stills. These books, loosely known as novelizations, have long been prized collectibles among movie fans. The first novelizations were not book-length stories; rather, they were short stories published in movie magazines such as *Movie Story.*

Book-length novelizations try to faithfully put into print what is seen and heard in the theater. A novelization is not the fiction or nonfiction book on which the movie is based but rather an original creation based on the movie itself. Thus, if you read the nonfiction book *Everything You Always Wanted to Know About Sex (But Were Afraid to Ask)* you will not find a single mention of Woody Allen, the director and star of the film of the same name. Similarly, the recent novelization of the movie Total Recall, written by Piers Anthony, is not the same story found in the book that the film is based on (*We Can Remember It for You Wholesale,* by Philip K. Dick).

In some cases, after a movie is released a publisher or studio will produce a special edition of the book the movie was based on containing graphic matter related to the film; however, collectors still seem to prefer novelizations over these modified original books. For instance, the original book upon which the film *Gone With the Wind* is based is of very little interest to movie collectors, yet almost any other item associated with the film is highly prized.

The one exception to this lack of interest in the original novel is in the case of an autographed copy of the original book—not autographed by the author, but autographed by the cast and crew of the movie. For example, a copy of the novel *Gone With the Wind* signed by 23 members of the film's cast and crew—including Clark Gable, Viven Leigh, Olivia de Havilland, Leslie Howard, and George Besselo (Reeves)—recently sold at auction for $20,000.

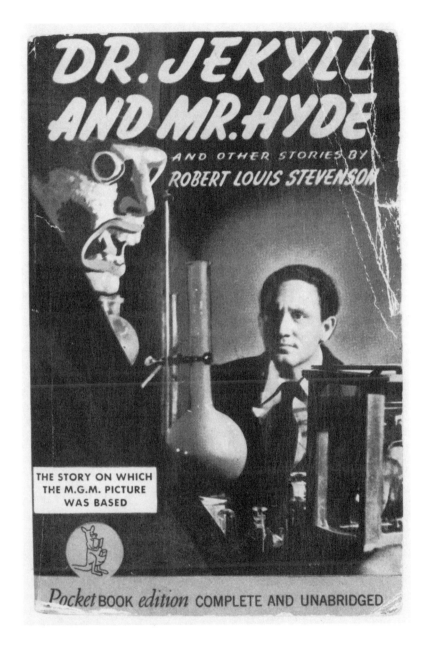

**Fig. 5-1.** Pocketbook edition of Robert Louis Stevenson's *Dr. Jekyll and Mr. Hyde,* released to support the 1941 MGM production of the same name.

Among the oldest and rarest novelizations are those published during the 1920s, such as the one for the Harold Lloyd film *The Freshman.* The novelization was a very popular form, and though the original idea for the medium was to provide people who had seen the movie with a way of continuing the experience, its popularity caused hundreds of thousands of people to see a film only *after* they had read the novelization of it.

Columbia Pictures
Presents
A Rastar Pictures Production

# GEORGE SEGAL
in
# THE BLACK BIRD
co-starring
## Stephane Audran

Screenplay by
**David Giler**
Story by
**Don M. Mankiewicz and Gordon Cotler**

A
Novelization
by
**Alexander
Edwards**

WARNER BOOKS
$1.25  76-766

**Fig. 5-2.** Paperback edition of *The Black Bird* (1975). Note that the screenplay, story, and novelization of this film were each written by a different person.

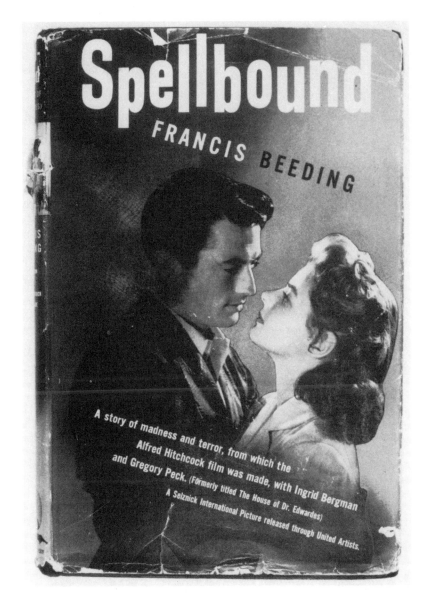

**Fig. 5-3.** Francis Beeding's novel *The House of Dr. Edwards* was retitled when it was re-released as a hardback book in conjunction with Alfred Hitchcock's film version entitled *Spellbound* (1945).

The World Publishing Company of Cleveland issued many ''complete and unabridged'' novels under their Forum Books and Tower Fiction imprints. These—like the Grosset and Dunlap Photoplay Editions—were illustrated motion-picture editions with dust jackets featuring the stars and black-and-white photographs from the films.

In the 1940s, Whitman Publishing Company published an Adventure and Mystery Series of hardcover novels featuring movie stars as the central characters. Marketed mainly to teenage girls, titles included *Ginger Rogers and the Riddle of the Scarlet Cloak, Judy Garland and the Hoodoo Costume, Shirley Temple and the Screaming Specter,* and

**Fig. 5-4.** Orson Welles' *Touch of Evil* (1958) inspired this re-release of Whit Masterson's novel.

*Bonita Granville and the Mystery of Star Island* (Bonita Granville played Nancy Drew on screen).

The advent of the paperback book during this same era matched up beautifully with movie novelizations. Sometimes selling for as little as 15 cents, these inexpensive, attractive, and portable "pocket books" continue to give film fans hours of movie-related entertainment.

**Fig. 5-5.** A collection of film novels and novelizations.

**Fig. 5-6.** Grosset and Dunlap novelizations.

Fig. 5-7. This overblown novelization of *Reptilicus* (1962) verged on the pornographic.

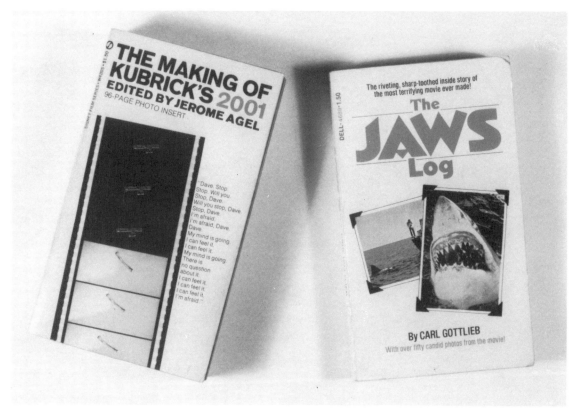

**Fig. 5-8.** "The Making of ..." movie books.

Three factors affect the value of a film book of this type: condition, story, and illustrations. First, the book itself must have a solid binding, no yellow pages, nothing torn, and no markings. Second, the story must read well, smoothly and dramatically giving a full, rich sense of the movie. Third, the book must contain numerous photographs of scenes from the movie. When these three criteria are met, the book closes in on the film experience and creates an attractive addition to any movie memorabilia collection.

Here are a few examples of 1991 prices for some mint condition novelizations: *Wings* (1927), $27.50; *The Last of Mrs. Cheyney* (1929), $20; *The Right of Way* (1928), $20; *Ceiling Zero* (1936), $20; *Gone With the Wind* (1939), $55; *The Misfits* (1961), $20; *Our Man Flint* (1966), $4; *Robin and the 7 Hoods* (1964), $5.

# Scripts

Script collecting has not reached full popularity among collectors. Though demand is low, most scripts are rare and worth quite a bit. Scripts are difficult to read and understand at first, but they provide a good means for developing an understanding of moviemaking

**Fig. 5-9.** A selection of original and reprinted scripts.

techniques since they describe camera angles, editing, and pacing, as well as action and dialogue.

Scripts are also useful in learning how a film has changed during production. The 1936 science fiction film *Things to Come* was originally two hours long, but current copies of the film run only one-and-a-half hours. Copies of the complete script for this film contain all the missing scenes and provide a view of what the movie was before it was subjected to the film editor's knife.

Scripts are pieces of movie material that were once held in the very hands of moviemakers. Actors learn their lines from scripts, set and costume designers develop their plans from them, and directors work from them or, at the very least, use them as a guide. Some scripts contain notations by the people who used them, making this sort of movie memorabilia particularly special.

At the end of the moviemaking process, a cast party is traditionally sponsored by the director. At these parties, the production personnel who made the movie often bring along their scripts, as souvenir albums, for everyone to sign. Such scripts are extraordinarily valuable. A leather-bound, gilt-stamped script for the film *Citizen Kane* (1940) recently sold for over $50,000.

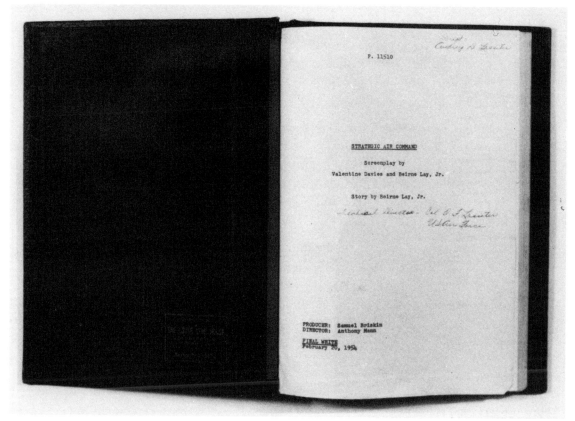

**Fig. 5-10.** Original and bound script from *Strategic Air Command* (1955).

Since scripts are protected by copyrights, they cannot be reproduced to increase supply for collector demand. But this same copyright has allowed for the publication of many anthologies and book series over the years. The Viking Press was at one time active with a series titled "The MGM Library of Film Scripts," which included single-volume screenplays for *Ninotchka, North by Northwest, Adam's Rib,* and *A Day at the Races,* among others. A recent trend has involved photocopying the actual pages from original Universal horror movie scripts, such as *Frankenstein,* in trade paperback editions accompanied by comments, photos, and interviews. In this way, the script reproduction gives the thrill of the original at the price of a copy.

To help you get a feel for what's out there and what you may have to part with to get it, here are some examples of 1991 prices for mint condition scripts: *Little Shop of Horrors* (1960), $35; *Ode to Billy Joe* (1976), $10; *Fireman Save My Child* (1932), $35; *The Crusades* (1935), $100; *Julius Caesar* (1953), $60; *Jungle Jim* (1948), $30; *Northwest Passage* (1940), $65; *White Christmas* (1954), $50; *Adventures of Captain Marvel* (1941), $250; *Air Raid Wardens* (1942), $150.

# Comics

Film is not the only medium that tells tales visually. Comics don't have music or movement, but they do show the sequential events and images of a film better than any other printed form. The first movie comics appeared as part of movie magazines. The film story was streamlined to only a few pages of panel graphics, mixed among the articles about film stars and upcoming features.

DC Comics published six issues of *Movie Comics* in 1939, each issue adapting as many as seven different films (such as *Gunga Din, Stagecoach, The Saint Strikes Back,* and *The Phantom Creeps.* Then the concept seemed to fade from interest until 1950 when several publishers launched magazines like *Motion Picture Comics* and *Film Stars Romances.* From that time on, you could "watch" a movie come to life again in comic book form. As a bonus, many old films were made in black-and-white, while their comic counterparts were in full color.

The value of these comics is extremely high, because old comics themselves are hugely popular collectibles. If you get a chance to acquire movie comics at reasonable prices, take advantage of the opportunity; it'll pay you back in terrific trading material. Some sample 1991 prices for comics in mint condition: *Dorothy Lamour No. 2* (1950), $10; *Destination Moon* (1950), $100; *Montana* (1950), E. Flynn, $50; *Gunman of Abilene* (1950), Rocky Lane, $35; *Last Outpost* (1951), R. Reagan, $80; *The Pride and the Passion* (1957), F. Sinatra, $8; *Ben-Hur* (1959), $10; *Dinosaurus* (1960), $6; *The Comancheros* (1961), J. Wayne, $20; *The Great Race* (1966), $5; *The Tomb of Ligeia* (1965), $2. (If you'd like to know more about collecting comics, read my book *Collector's Guide to Comic Books,* also published by Wallace-Homestead.)

Much like the comics, Big Little Books (BLBs) adapted film stories with either art or actual photographs assembled into palm-sized books with cardboard covers. BLBs featured many famous and favorite movie comedy and adventure characters such as Mickey Mouse, Tarzan, and Popeye. Throughout the 1930s, major films were broken down into 300-page "storyboards" with a photo on every page opposing a paragraph or two of story.

The Whitman Publishing Company of Racine, Wisconsin, produced a mini-library of BLBs, including *David Copperfield* (1935) with photos of W.C. Fields. The Saalfield Publishing Company produced books like *It Happened One Night* (1935) (with photos of Clark Gable and Claudette Colbert) and *The Lost Patrol* (1934) (featuring Boris Karloff and Victor McLaglen). One prized BLB is *Tom Mix in Terror Trail* from the 1933 Universal Picture of the same name. Other stars featured in this BLB series were Jackie Cooper, Shirley Temple, and Our Gang. As a bonus, one BLB featured a double bill of photos from the Johnny Weissmuller films *Tarzan, the Ape Man* (1932) and *Tarzan and His Mate* (1934).

While there are many people who feel that a book is a book and a movie is a movie, the two media have a lot to share. They both tell stories and they both promise hours of quality entertainment for every movie fan.

**Fig. 5-11.** A selection of movies adapted to comic books.

# CHAPTER 6

# Movie Magazines, Programs, and Press Books

**A**S YOU MAY HAVE NOTICED, information and entertainment media tend to support one another. For example, "The Lux Radio Theatre" supported movies by presenting Hollywood stars and directors over the nation's airwaves. Later it evolved into the "The Lux Video Theatre." The Lone Ranger appeared in many media—the comics, radio, television, and film. The actress Fanny Brice began her career in vaudeville, moved to radio, and then appeared occasionally in movies, such as *Crime Without Passion* (1934). In each case, one form of entertainment connects to another in the public awareness like links in a chain.

## Movie Magazines

One of the most successful joinings of media is that of movies and magazines. In decades past, a sizable section of newsstand racks was given over to movie star publications. The legendary town of celluloid dreams and these stellar periodicals of awed and affirmative support complemented each other magnificently. There are three basic types of movie magazines:

- Technical industry publications, like *Variety* and *The Hollywood Reporter*
- Scholarly film analysis periodicals, like *Films in Review* and *Film Comment*
- Movie fan magazines, like *Movie Classic* and *Filmfax*

The best known of the early trade papers is *The Moving Picture World*, published from 1907 through 1928. Closely related to the trade papers are the house organs published by individual producers or distributors to promote their films and contract stars. Among these are *The Edison Kinetogram* and MGM's *The Lion's Roar*. Issues of these publi-

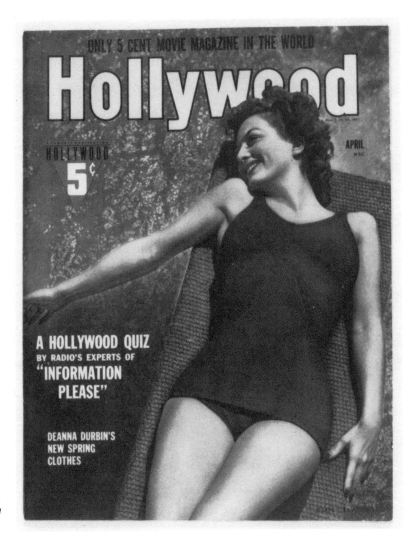

**Fig. 6-1.** Photo cover of Joan Crawford for *Hollywood* (April 1940).

cations are valuable as pioneer ventures in film promotion but are usually of interest only to libraries and museums who need to have complete historical reference material.

The magazines most sought by collectors of movie memorabilia are publications like *Photoplay, Shadowland, Hollywood,* and *Silver Screen*. These movie magazines (sometimes called fan magazines) kept a constant parade of cinema fans going to the movies year in and year out. In return the movies kept folks going back to the magazines by supplying the publications with photos and features designed to make moviegoers sit up and take notice of the "news" from Hollywood. At their prime, many of these publications had circulations approaching 500,000, each issue jammed full of Hollywood gossip.

The premiere of the most successful movie magazines came with the establishment of the "star" system. The movie public was fascinated by the early darlings of the screen,

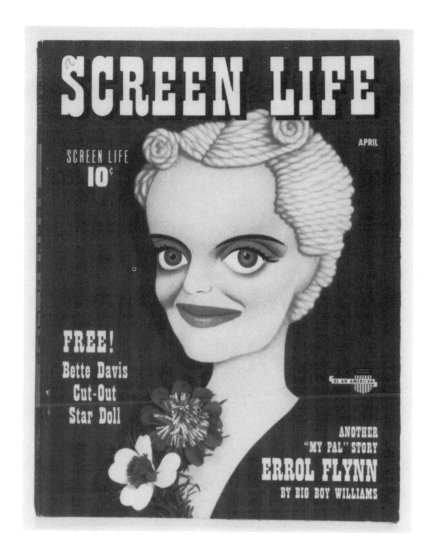

Fig. 6-2. Caricature cover of Bette Davis for *Screen Life* (April 1941). This issue also offered cutout paper dolls of Bette.

and faithfully devoted to the likes of Richard Barthelmess, Charlie Chaplin, and Lillian Gish. *Photoplay* and *Picture Play* were among the first of the magazines to cash in on the story of Hollywood.

In 1911 came *Motion Picture Story*, followed by *Moving Picture Stories* in 1913, which recounted the glamour of the movie world for even more readers. The ever-increasing market led to *Photoplay Journal*, first published in 1916, and *Photoplay World*, introduced in 1917. In 1923, *Screenland* appeared. Its pages were full of attractive professional photos and revealing stories about current matinee idols such as Rudolph Valentino, Lon Chaney, and Douglas Fairbanks.

By this time, the 7″ × 9″ magazines began using eye-catching covers produced using the newly developed four-color printing process. The colorful covers featured a full-face

**Fig. 6-3.** *Hollywood Glamor Girls* No. 1. (1955)—the cover says it all.

painting of a popular film star such as Gloria Swanson, Harold Lloyd, or Tom Mix. Generally speaking, collectors feel that the golden age of movie fan magazines falls between 1929 and 1940. The American public at this time was obsessed with stories about movie stars, and "exclusive" photographs of the stars at home, in nightclubs, on the set, and at movie premieres sold magazines by the thousands.

*Modern Screen* magazine was introduced in 1930 with 200 pages containing dozens of striking studio portraits of movie performers, many scenes from movies, and casual on-stage or at-poolside photographs of the stars. The magazine carried approximately 100 excellent pictures in an average issue as well as at least one novelization. (One magazine, *Movie Story,* specialized in nothing but novelizations of the current popular films.)

**Fig. 6-4.** *Photoplay* cover of Rita Hayworth (October 1949).

In many cases, it is not so much the content of the magazine as the celebrity on the cover that determines an issue's value to many collectors. Attractive glamour portraits, produced by the likes of Clarence Bull and George Hurrell, masters of cinema photography, graced the covers of magazines throughout the 1940s. Savvy collectors pay attention to a magazine's cover *and* to its contents—which include a host of wonderful articles, ads, and novelties such as paper-doll cutouts.

Intriguing stories featured within an issue were often advertised on the cover with large-letter banner headlines. "Bette Davis Faces Sorrow," "Hollywood's Unmarried Husbands and Wives," "The Real Truth about John Gilbert's Death," "How I Keep My Figure" (by Betty Grable), and "The Madcap Love of the Errol Flynns."

The December 1939 issue of *Modern Screen* would be an attractive addition to any collection. That issue includes an article on George Brent ("He Loves Them and Leaves

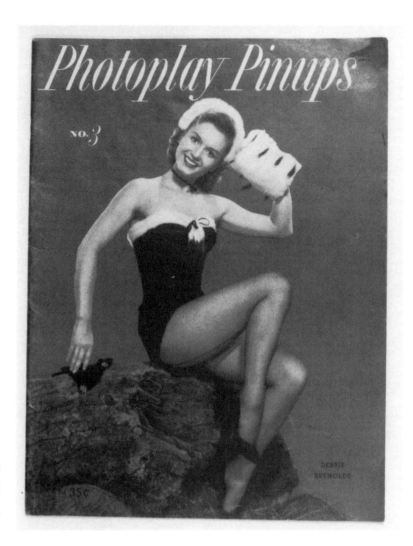

**Fig. 6-5.** *Photoplay Pinups* with Debbie Reynolds presents page after page of color pinups of big name stars.

Them''); a story about Robert Taylor's neighbors; and features on Deanna Durbin, Henry Fonda, Greta Garbo, and Gene Autry. Each article is accompanied by glorious studio photos. One feature in this issue describes George Raft as the "Good-hearted Gangster," another presents Jane Wyman giving step-by-step instructions for a refreshing facial, and another shows you the homes of Barbara Stanwyck, Tyrone Power, Clark Gable, and Nelson Eddy. All this material, plus over 60 additional photographs of Hollywood stars, is packed into a single issue of a movie magazine that originally sold for the bargain price of 10 cents (today's value: approximately $30).

Many major movies were advertised in full color and given full-page treatments in the movie magazines. The typical movie fan magazine contained four or five such ads, so collecting fan magazines can be a relatively easy and inexpensive way of collecting

**Fig. 6-6.** Early issue of *Photoplay* (September 1924) with Colleen Moore cover illustration.

poster art. Ads in the magazines mirrored the obsession with the Hollywood ideal of flawless beauty obtainable through star-endorsed products: Joan Crawford for Lustre Creme shampoo, Barbara Stanwyck for Max Factor makeup, Cathy O'Donnell for Jergens hand lotion, and Ann Sheridan for Lux soap (see Fig. 6-13).

Over the years, ads with movie-star endorsements have become increasingly popular among even casual movie enthusiasts. Such ads are often found at flea markets and antique shows backed by cardboard and covered with plastic. Stacked in boxes, they are usually filed under the name of the star, ready for some new owner to discover and buy them.

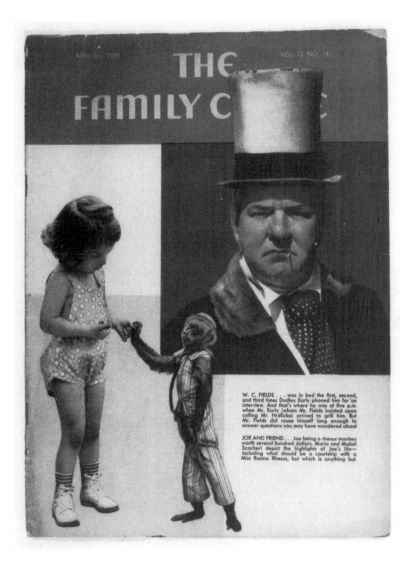

Fig. 6-7. *Family Circle* was a weekly giveaway at the grocery checkout counter. This issue shows W. C. Fields as he appeared in *David Copperfield* (1935).

There is one drawback to the contents of movie magazines: the best cinema action scenes are not found on their pages, since a photo had to be reduced in size to illustrate an article. Thus, scenes from actual films are often neglected in favor of posed studio portraits.

You'll encounter many magazines from the 1950s that feature Marilyn Monroe, Tony Curtis, James Dean, Elizabeth Taylor, Debbie Reynolds, and Natalie Wood. The list of popular magazines that displayed these performers is almost endless. *Life, Look,* and *The Saturday Evening Post* all presented in-depth views of stars and reviews of films. Such publications are invaluable resources in the study of media, publicity, and hype.

**Fig. 6-8.** A selection of contemporary movie magazines. The basics are still there: movie promotion and fun.

From this flurry of 1950s movie promotion came my fondly remembered "monster mags." *Famous Monsters of the Filmland* and *Mad Monsters* offered an insight into the special effects and makeup used in gory horror flicks. Readers loved them and still do, as this tradition continues with current publications such as *Gorezone* and *Cinefex*.

Similar to the above, but on a higher intellectual level, are the "serious" film periodicals. Issues of *American Cinematographer* and *Film Culture* offer interesting information on the more technical aspects of moviemaking and movie history.

There is no accurate record of just how many film periodicals have been published since the cinema began. The number is probably over a thousand. All have some value in recording contemporary cinema and documenting film history, and the majority are or will become collector's items, someday.

A special light still burns deep within the hearts of true movie fans for their favorite movie magazines. The local library never subscribed to most of them, and tons of old magazines were pulped for the World War II paper drives. Consequently, today there is a limited supply of this material. Prices for even the most ordinary of these peeks behind

(*continued on page 100*)

**Fig. 6-9.** Magazine advertisement for *All This and Heaven Too* (1940).

**Fig. 6-10.** Magazine advertisement for *War Nurse* (1932).

**Fig. 6-11.** Magazine advertisement for *Lightnin'* (1932).

**Fig. 6-12.** Magazine advertisement for *Chandu the Magician* (1932).

**Fig. 6-13.** Ann Sheridan promoting Lux Soap (1940 ad).

**Fig. 6-14.** Magazine advertisement for *Movie Crazy* (1932).

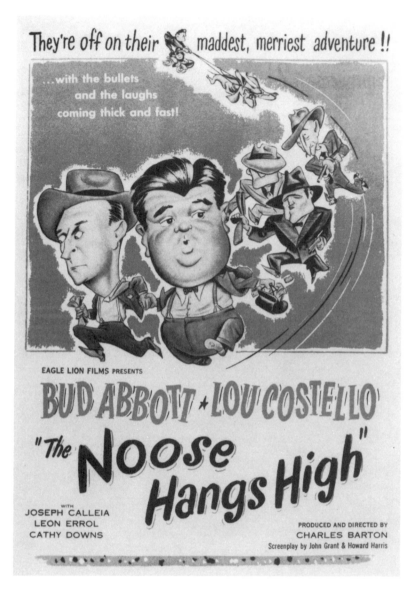

**Fig. 6-15.** Magazine advertisement for *The Noose Hangs High* (1948).

**Fig. 6-16.** Magazine advertisement for *The Pirate* (1948).

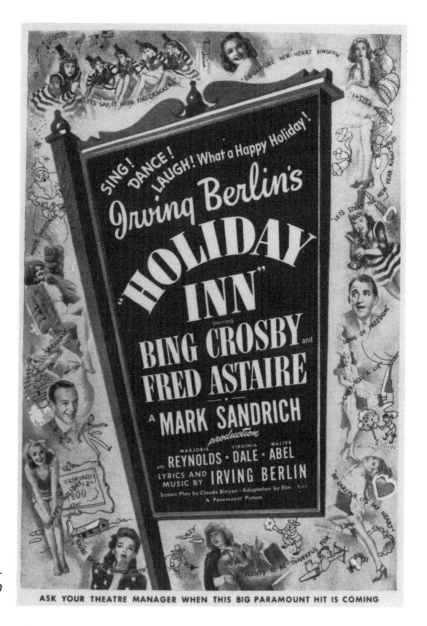

**Fig. 6-17.** Magazine advertisement for *Holiday Inn* (1942).

the scenes in Hollywood—which originally sold for as little as a nickel and as much as a quarter—are usually over $10 today, providing the magazine is complete and in nice condition. For example, here are some late-1990 prices for various magazine issues in mint condition: *Screen Romances,* January 1937, $20; *Movie Story,* October 1937, $25; *Modern Screen,* May 1934, $25; *Screenland,* November 1938, $18; *Movie Mirror,* August 1935, $15; *Life,* April 1956, J. Mansfield, $10; *Life,* January 1955, G. Garbo, $15; *Shriek*

**Fig. 6-18.** A selection of movie program books.

*No. 1* (1965), $20; *Famous Monsters #33*, $12; *Famous Monsters #66*, $6; *Screen Thrills Illustrated #7*, $5; *Photoplay,* October 1923, $25; *Picture Play,* April 1925, $25.

# Program Books

When D. W. Griffith's *The Clansman (Birth of a Nation)* opened in 1915, the theater gave its patrons an elegant souvenir program book containing a story synopsis and portraits of the leading players. Over the years, such souvenir programs have been handed out or sold for a dime to a dollar. Many have become cherished collectibles.

Like commemoratives of the film's premiere, each program has full-color illustrations, credits for the cast and technical personnel, a brief plot rundown, and articles on the production and the personalities involved. By the end of the 1940s, theater programs were all but forgotten, printed only for special Hollywood events, grand openings, and anniversaries. Then, in the mid-1950s, with advances in technicolor, cinemascope, and other exciting film innovations designed to compete with the increasing popularity of television, program books returned to theater lobbies. Recent popular films, such as *Star*

*Wars* and the revival of Abel Gance's *Napoleon,* have continued this tradition of movie collectibles. A program book is a rare and wonderful addition to any collection of movie memorabilia. It symbolizes the inauguration of a new work of art in the Hollywood gallery of stars. Here are a few examples of late-1990 prices for programs in mint condition: *Gone With the Wind* (1939), $250; *Star Wars* (1977), $25; *All Quiet on the Western Front* (1930), $75; *Hunchback of Notre Dame* (1923), $125; *The Wizard of Oz* (1939), $1400; *Metropolis* (1927), $1980.

# Press Books

Like the movies themselves, press books were an art form that drew upon the talents of many different people with as many different and highly developed skills. Press books were expensive to make. A variety of people added their creativity to the process: gifted writers, layout artists, editors, photographers, highly imaginative "idea" people, printers, and promoters.

Before the release date of a major film, the publicity departments of movie studios would send press books out to exhibitors, theater owners, and managers. In the 1930s and 1940s, press books were made to promote A (first feature) movies. As a rule, B (budget) pictures did not have to be promoted by press books. The main attraction or feature was the thing that sold the tickets, aided by the *idea* that there was going to be a second feature-length movie plus a cartoon, newsreel, and trailer.

The unique art form of the press book makes such books handsome and enviable additions to any collection of movie memorabilia. The press book contains prepared reviews for busy editors, interview material, special articles stressing various points in the movie, thumbnail biographies, radio spots, ideas for contests, and sample ads with blank spaces provided for a local theater to add its name, playing times, and dates. All of this material was designed to arouse interest in a movie in order to drive people to the box office. Since many of the items in a press book were designed to be cut out and sent to local newspapers to promote a feature film, complete and uncut books are now among the most difficult and valuable memorabilia to collect.

Press books also contained complete descriptions of the various promotional graphics (posters, lobby cards, and so on) that could be purchased or rented—for as little as 5 or 10 cents—to help promote the movie. Today, this detailed record gives poster collectors a clear guide to the design and availability (at the time) of promotional material. The lobbies, window cards, and one-sheet posters were often saved by the theater manager in case of a return engagement, and press books were shelved for a time; however, because such items were difficult to handle and store, they were often eventually discarded.

Early press books also offered a listing of color slides to be used to promote upcoming films. What we now call "Previews of Coming Attractions" or trailers (because they trailed along behind the feature film) originally consisted of scenes mounted on slides that were inserted into the projector and cast upon the screen. These slides contained a dramatic scene from an upcoming film or the title and name of the star performers in the

# REWARD!!!
## WANTED - FINGER PRINTS

to match these found on the secret

plans of the

# Black Dragon

These are the finger prints of the Black Dragon.
See how closely yours match them.

Then go and see "G-MEN VS. THE
BLACK DRAGON", Republic's thrilling,
exciting and nerve-tingling serial of the
Jap menace at our door! With Rod Cam-
eron, Roland Got, Constance Worth and a
great cast! Coming to the

# THEATRE IMPRINT

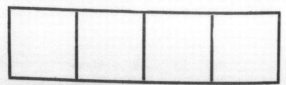

**PLACE YOUR FINGER PRINTS HERE**

Fig. 6-19. Press book promotional
material for *G-Men vs. the Black
Dragon* serial (1943).

THE **GREEN ARCHER** CLUB

| 8 | 1 |
|---|---|
| 9 | 2 |
| 10 | 3 |
| 11 | 4 |
| 12 | 5 |
| 13 | 6 |
| 14 | 7 |
| 15 | FREE |

NAME

See 14 Chapters of 'The Green Archer'
and have this card punched each week.
Then present card at door and see last
chapter absolutely FREE!

**STATE THEATRE**

Fig. 6-20. Press book art for punch card of *The Green Archer* (1940). Patrons who came each week and saw chapters 1 through 14 of this serial were admitted to the final chapter at no charge.

film. Slides from this period are very rare and fragile. Most of them were made on glass and were discarded after the film opened, their usefulness over.

Other unusual items presented in press books included comic strips, maze games, and discount cards used to lure children to serial chapter plays. Many movie memorabilia items—such as napkins, photos, buttons, and badges—have been promoted in press books as a way to provide moviegoers with small mementos of their film-viewing experiences. Many special and entertaining collections have been built up over the years consisting of these movie giveaways.

Feature stories in press books, including full biographies of the stars, were almost always total fabrications; audiences seemed to want to believe that the actual lives of the stars were as interesting and glamorous as those of the characters they portrayed in the movies. Many of the erroneous details spread by such press book accounts continue to appear in today's ''official'' biographies of the stars, retold and embroidered for a new generation of film fans. For example, contrary to widespread belief, Bogart never said, ''Drop the gun, Louie,'' or ''Tennis, anyone,'' or even ''Play it again, Sam.'' (In the latter case, what he said was, ''You played it for her. You can play it for me. If she can stand it, I can. Play it!'')

The content of press books varied, but their purpose was always the same: to stir

**Fig. 6-21.** Contemporary press kit for *Star Trek IV: The Voyage Home* (1987).

up interest in the film. To do this, press books provided ready-made articles and feature stories designed to generate enthusiasm, while being very easy to insert into newspaper columns and entertainment pages. In addition to providing a quick synopsis of the film story, a feature article might offer ''inside stories'' about how the film was made or telling details about the lives of the movie's leading personalities. Most of these details never happened, but they were part of a rich fantasy designed to whet the audience's appetite and win attention for the film.

A few examples of 1991 prices for press books in mint condition might be helpful here to give you an idea of the wide range of values for these books: *Apache Rifles* (1964), $2; *Beneath the Planet of the Apes* (1970), $6; *Ace Drummond* (1936), $15; *Chisum* (1970), J. Wayne, $6; *Deadfall* (1968), $4; *Adventures of Mark Twain* (1944), $25; *Godzilla vs. the Thing* (1964), $15; *Public Pigeon No. 1* (1957), R. Skelton, $10; *George Raft Story* (1961), $10; *Elephant Walk* (1954), $25; *Across the Pacific* (1942), H. Bogart, $125.

The press book has now been replaced by the press kit (see Fig. 6-21), a folder holding the following: pages of cast and technical credits; production information; a synopsis; biographical information on the players, director, and producer; and a set of still photographs. But for a time during the golden age of Hollywood, press books were a focal point for almost every aspect of moviemaking.

So, while many press books, programs, and movie magazines don't always tell the truth about a movie, they inspire film fans to treasure their time in the theater—and they keep 'em coming back for more.

# CHAPTER 7

# Soundtracks

**M**OVIE MUSIC IS DRAMATIC MUSIC. Songs are sung to capture a moment like "When You Wish Upon a Star" from *Pinocchio* (1940) and "Swingin' on a Star" from *Going My Way* (1944). Songs are part of grand production numbers like "Broadway Melody" in *Singin' in the Rain* (1952) and "Doing the Timewarp" in *The Rocky Horror Picture Show*.

Movie musicals such as *High Society* (1956), *Robin and the 7 Hoods* (1964), and *The Little Mermaid* (1989) provide many hit tunes that inspire people to purchase the movie soundtracks in some form. Each symphonic soundtrack conjures up scenes from the film and a sense of romantic adventure.

Although over 60 years have gone by, the songs that *The Jazz Singer* brought to the screen in theaters all over the country have become an important part of the artistic and musical heritage of America. And it's hard to separate "Somewhere Over the Rainbow" from its scene in *The Wizard of Oz,* just as it's hard to imagine the flashback sequence from *Casablanca* without Max Steiner's moving score.

## Three Categories

In terms of content, movie music albums can be divided according to three broad categories: major musical themes, works of noted film score composers, and music performed by personalities.

*Major musical themes.* These are examples of film music that has had a great impact on the public. Examples include "As Time Goes By" from *Casablanca,* the shark theme from *Jaws,* and the use of "Thus Spake Zarasthrustra" in *2001: A Space Odyssey.*

*Works of noted film score composers.* Several professional composers have developed careers of writing and conducting excellent film music over several decades. Examples include Erich Wolfgang Korngold's music for *The Sea Hawk* and *King's Row,*

Fig. 7-1. Recomposed film music anthology conducted by the music's original composer, Miklós Rózsa.

Bernard Herrmann's music for *Psycho* and *North by Northwest,* and Miklos Rozsa's music for *El Cid* and *Young Bess.*

Most collectors concentrate on composers, the talented people who devote their careers to fixing the forms and developing creative styles within the forms. Here is a list of popular film composers:

Elmer Bernstein                Miklos Rozsa
Hugo Friedhofer                Max Steiner
Jerry Goldsmith                Dimitri Tiomkin
Bernard Herrmann               Franz Waxman
Erich Wolfgang Korngold        John Williams
Henri Mancini                  Victor Young
Alfred Newman

Rarities present few problems. If they can be found at all, they will appear in old record bargain bins, or at local record collector conventions.

*Music performed by personalities.* Well-known musical performers have in many cases lent their voices and skills to a film's theme or a musical number. Examples include

**Fig. 7-2.** Original soundtrack recording for *Obsession* (1976), composed and conducted by Bernard Herrmann.

Gene Kelly's song and dance from *Singin' in the Rain,* Shirley Temple's version of "On the Good Ship Lollipop," and Bing Crosby's crooning "Moonlight Becomes You" and "White Christmas" in several popular films.

Movie soundtrack collecting is a specialized field of movie memorabilia collecting, and it's a special category of record collecting, too. There are thousands of collectors of movie music, each devoted to his or her favorite films and composers. Collectors of soundtracks often collect and value their items not because of a specific film title but rather because of the film score composer, and today there exists a large and continuously growing market for recorded film music by the composers Alex North, John Williams, Miklos Rozsa, and Bernard Herrmann, among others.

Movie soundtracks are a collectible within a collectible. They require special insight, knowledge, and care. The value of movie soundtrack records is determined by title, condition (both the record and the jacket), and, of course, supply and demand. A reissue of a record is worth less than the original, but not much less because advances in sound technology have actually improved the quality of many recordings.

For the classic movie musicals of the 1930s and 1940s there are very few record albums available. (One of the earliest of these musicals is Rozsa's *Jungle Book,* which was narrated by Sabu and appeared in binders containing several 78 rpm disks.) It is

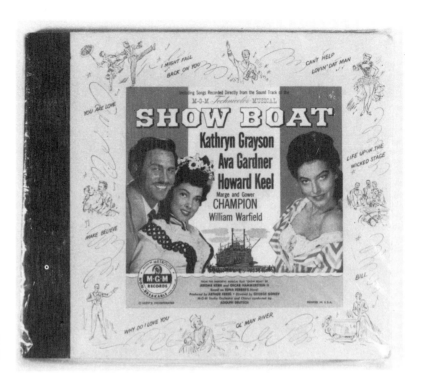

**Fig. 7-3.** Soundtrack album of 78 rpm records from *Show Boat* (1951).

interesting to note that the record jacket came into general use at this time, appearing on Rozsa's music for Hitchcock's *Spellbound* in 1945.

When you purchase a film soundtrack you acquire an audio device that will allow you to relive moments of the film as often as you like. There are only a limited number of movie music recordings, so you can, in many cases, build a complete collection of those albums that interest you. General interest in soundtrack collecting only began as recently as the mid-1950s with the introduction of long-playing (LP) record albums of "hi-fi" and later "stereo" sound.

As is the case with movie posters, this book only examines those records that were issued in the United States, or at least widely distributed here.

# Examining Some Terms

## Soundtracks

The term *soundtrack* has been badly abused by collectors and record manufacturers. Strictly speaking, a genuine soundtrack recording is a recording taken directly from the film's playback disc, including everything acoustical from the orchestra's soundstage, rather than from the film's production stage.

**Fig. 7-4.** Movie music is available in many media: 7" reel tapes, cassette tapes, LP record albums, and compact discs.

From the very beginning of sound movies some of the music and songs used were recorded in regular soundstage studios, away from the other, noisier aspects of movie production. In the early days records were not made from the soundtracks, and the original playback disc has often either been destroyed, given away, or lost.

Remember the scene in *Singin' in the Rain* where Debbie Reynolds appears to be dubbing in the voice of Jean Hagen? This dubbing of Debbie's voice over Jean's picture is produced from a ''playback'' disc, and like the orchestration recorded on its playback disc, it is added to the movie after the film strip had run through the camera. It is therefore the soundtrack. If compared to what you hear in the theater when the movie was shown, this ''playback'' version will sound quite different. Remember, the theater-experience music resulting from the film strip and including the dialogue and sound effects is *not* the film's soundtrack.

To make matters even more confusing, most soundtracks are made up either of the prerecorded music tracks or of completely rerecorded selections from the score. Many records released are original soundtracks and many others are compilations of songs or music actually recorded in a studio either by the original artist or by someone else. Those tracks recorded in a studio do not include incidental sound effects or dialogue from the

**Fig. 7-5.** LP soundtrack album for *Sodom and Gomorrah* (1963).

film. Those done after the film was made often contain altered lyrics. Those done by other than original artists often present completely different (and sometimes intriguing) arrangements. Of these types of movie recordings, the original soundtrack is the most valuable whereas records recorded by artists other than the original artists are the least valuable. And speaking of value, here are a few 1991 sample prices to give you an idea of what you might have to pay for soundtracks in mint condition: *Deadfall* (1968), J. Barry, $25; *Golden Voyage Of Sinbad* (1974), M. Rozsa, $10; *Name of the Rose* (1988), J. Horner, $16; *Obsession* (1976), B. Herrmann, $16; *Taras Bulba* (1962), F. Waxman, $37; *Sand Pebbles* (1966), J. Goldsmith, $40; *Duck You Sucker* (1972), E. Morricone, $18; *Hatari!* (1962), H. Mancini, $15; *Gone With the Wind* (1939), M. Steiner, $7; *Duel in the Sun* (1946), D. Tiomkin, $55; *Swimmer* (1968), M. Hamlisch, $40; *Sons of Katie Elder* (1965), E. Bernstein, $55; *Fitzwilly* (1967), J. Williams, $17; *Spirit of St. Louis* (1957), F. Waxman, $10.

The collecting network for movie music consists of an intricate web of mail-order dealers, rare-record stores, nostalgia shops, soundtrack traders, and mobile investors who buy on a shoestring and sell for a profit in order to afford to add to their own collections.

Fig. 7-6. A compilation of songs sung by Marilyn in her many films.

Movie music is increasingly important for collectors, and many different kinds of records of many different quality levels have appeared on the market. The great variety of recordings affects values for collectors and collections. It is therefore important to know some of the terms and facts that concern movie music recordings in order to know what to get and to know what you're getting.

## Reissues

Many albums have never gone "out of print," which translates into a low value for original issues even though they may be 40 years old. As is the case for 8″ × 10″ stills, for recordings there are copies of copies and duplicates of duplicates. In the record industry, it is a fairly common practice for a major record producer who finds that it is no longer profitable to continue a particular title to drop the title from the list. However, because there may still be some demand which may make distribution profitable for a smaller company, the smaller company will press a copy. That copy is known as a reissue.

**Fig. 7-7.** Cinemascope soundtrack for *State Fair* (1962).

## Jackets

The record jacket—the outside cover of an album, usually displaying some artwork and providing pertinent information about the album—is considered to be an essential part of a soundtrack album. A record without the dust jacket is considered by many collectors to be just a piece of plastic; likewise, an album cover without the record is hardly worth considering at all.

# Compact Disc Recordings

There's been a recent revolution in collecting movie soundtracks. Most people have been listening to recorded music in essentially the same way for nearly 110 years. The modern LP record stores music in the form of jagged grooves, which correspond to the sound waves that are picked up by microphones at the time of the live performance. The electrical signals from these microphones are amplified until they are powerful enough to drive a cutting stylus, or needle. This stylus cuts the groove in a "master disc," which is then used to produce the vinyl LP record played on the phonograph.

Fig. 7-8. A collection of show tunes performed by a couple of song and dance men—not a soundtrack but collectible and lots of fun.

All this recording equipment employs an analog system of documenting sound. The groove in the record is analogous to the sound wave pattern that it is supposed to represent, but even the best LP has several disadvantages. For one thing, it is subject to wear. No matter how carefully you handle records, your phonograph needle will eventually wear away the more delicate groove undulations. In addition, an LP cannot handle the complete dynamic range between the loudest and softest sounds in any musical selection; and there is often the background hiss of surface noise.

The compact (digital) disc (CD) measures only 12 centimeters in diameter and can play more than an hour of music on one side. Digital information is stored beneath the surface of the disc in the form of microscopic depressions, or pits. The pattern of these pits is molded into the disc in a continuous spiral design.

Nothing touches the surface of the disc as it is played. A laser beam strikes the pattern of pits, and reflection angles are determined by whether the light strikes a pit or the area where there is no pit. These variations in the reflected laser beam represent the 0's and 1's of the digital (binary) code. A photocell converts the light variations into electrical signals that are amplified and converted back to analog signals that generate the sound.

There are many benefits associated with compact discs. A compact disc provides information in a form that is more compact than that of an LP record. The range of the music is more "complete" and is sharper. Also, discs are more durable and the recording technique has extremely low harmonic distortion, that is, less wow and flutter.

All of this information is somewhat technical, but it will also help you understand the visual and audio portions of the laser videodisc discussion in the next chapter. Welcome to tomorrow!

# CHAPTER 8

# Films and Videos

RECENTLY I MET A MAN who had converted his spare bedroom into a mini-theater where he shows 16mm films to his friends. I know of seven or eight such "home theaters" in the central Ohio area. One fellow shows Cinerama films in his living room! Imagine three 35mm projectors operating at the same time in your house or apartment, filling a 35-foot screen with films like *How the West Was Won* (1963).

Collecting movies is the most basic form of amassing movie memorabilia—and lately the most popular. The movies themselves are the ultimate collectible. And the recent video and laser disc revolution has made it possible for you to own and view almost any sound film produced in the last 70 years, as well as a nice selection of silent features and comedy shorts subjects.

Film collecting is also the area of movie memorabilia that is going through the greatest transition. Once, creaky 8mm projectors displayed silent movies in collectors' dark cellars. Now, Dolby-like stereo laser discs can present top box-office features on big-screen TV's as little as six months after the films premiere in the theaters.

## Collecting Films

Of all hobbies associated with the motion picture none is more complex than that of collecting films. With the video revolution taking place, more and more people are acquiring videotapes and videodiscs of both old and new feature films. It's doubtful that any of the tapes will increase in value any time soon, but few collectors these days would consider buying a standard 8mm or super 8mm (Super8) version of their favorite films for $150 or more when they can have a videotape of the same feature for as little as $20.

The 8mm film stock is just of the film gauges on which films are available. Theatrical feature-length films generally are shot on 35mm stock. When these films are released

**Fig. 8-1.** Classic 35mm movie camera and a couple of its best subjects, Laurel and Hardy.

nontheatrically (meaning for home use) they are "reduced" to 16mm. For standard 8mm and Super8, the films are reduced further.

Quite logically, 8mm celluloid film stock is made by slicing 16mm stock in half, and 16mm film comes from slicing 35mm film stock in half after first cutting away the sprocket hole area.

Many beginners want to know what "super" means in Super8. There is no change in film size; rather, the difference involves a change in format that increases the picture size. With Super8 film, the sprocket holes are made smaller, spaced farther apart, and moved closer to the edge of the film, thus enlarging the picture area by one-third and improving projectability.

The major problem facing film collectors is print quality. One distributor may have a beautiful 35mm original print of a film, make a new 16mm negative from it, and sell high-quality prints struck directly from the 16mm negative. However, because this film is in the public domain, there is absolutely nothing to stop an unscrupulous dealer from making a 16mm negative from a 16mm print acquired from the first dealer and then selling 16mm prints made from that inferior negative. The process can go on and on until the quality of the picture is sludge-like. And a similar process can occur with dupes of dupes of videotapes, until the final dupe is the guy who buys such a copy, never knowing that a superior copy exists.

There is no solution to the problem of reproduction quality. Film collectors must learn which dealers to trust and which to bypass. One source of such information can be found in collector publications like *Classic Images*, which provides enthusiasts with a wealth of information and a wide selection of dealers. In addition to dealer information,

Fig. 8-2. A master of the silent adventure film, Douglas Fairbanks, Sr.

this publication offers articles on film history, information on new releases, film and book reviews, and features on technical tips.

As far as color films are concerned, there is also the problem of film stock. Scratching and fading are a fact of life with most color films.

The emulsion side of a film is generally dull, and the base side is shiny. Emulsion scratches are different from base scratches in that base scratches will appear black because they reflect the light, while emulsion scratches can be white, yellow, or green, depending on how deep the scratch penetrates the emulsion surface.

The only prints that will not fade are Black and White, IB (Imbabision) Tech, and Kodachrome, a reversal stock that can be made from another print rather than from a negative.

The best film for most purposes today is manufactured domestically by Eastman

**Fig. 8-3.** Standard film gauges (left to right): 70mm, 35mm, 16mm, Super8mm, and 8mm, shown here at half normal size.

Kodak. The controls used both in making and processing this film have been refined to a high degree of excellence. Fuji film from Japan is also of superior quality, but it is not as commonly used in the United States.

Eastman color print film is known as "low fade" stock. Over time, the chemical compositon of the film will change, resulting in all but the red colors fading away from the emulsion. This means that after a certain number of years your beautiful full-color 16mm or 8mm print of *Life with Father* (1947) will turn an unappealing red.

Eastman stock can turn in 10 to 30 years. Knowing the stock code of a film can tell you how old the film stock is. It's important to note that it doesn't matter how old the movie itself is; what matters here is the age of the film stock on which the movie is printed. For example, a print of *Life with Father* struck on new Eastman film in the year 1968 might still look great today, but it will be expected to fade by 1998.

Fortunately, you can get an estimate of the age of a print by looking for a code on

| Year | Symbol | Year | Symbol | Year | Symbol |
|------|--------|------|--------|------|--------|
| 1950 | △+ | 1967 | □△ | 1984 | △□△ |
| 1951 | ○+ | 1968 | ++ | 1985 | □○△ |
| 1952 | □+ | 1969 | + | 1986 | △○△ |
| 1953 | +△ | 1970 | △+ | 1987 | □△△ |
| 1954 | +○ | 1971 | ○+ | 1988 | ++△ |
| 1955 | +□ | 1972 | □+ | 1989 | ×+△ |
| 1956 | ○ | 1973 | +△ | 1990 | △+△ |
| 1957 | □ | 1974 | +○ | 1991 | ×+× |
| 1958 | △ | 1975 | +□ | 1992 | □+△ |
| 1959 | ○○ | 1976 | ○ | 1993 | +△△ |
| 1960 | □□ | 1977 | □ | 1994 | +○△ |
| 1961 | △△ | 1978 | △ | 1995 | +□△ |
| 1962 | ○□ | 1979 | ○○ | 1996 | ×○△ |
| 1963 | ○△ | 1980 | □□ | 1997 | ×□△ |
| 1964 | △□ | 1981 | △△ | 1998 | ×△△ |
| 1965 | □○ | 1982 | ○□× | 1999 | ○×△ |
| 1966 | △○ | 1983 | ×△× | 2000 | □□△ |

the edge of the film strip that will tell you the year of its manufacture. In this way, you can estimate when the color print will begin to turn red. For example, the code for 1968 is ++. And for 1969, it's +. The year symbol, designating the year of manufacture, is incorporated into the edgeprint legend of almost all Eastman stock. These symbols, shown in the accompanying Chart, may be either open or closed up.

Keep in mind that 10 to 30 years is only an estimate. There is no certain indication when the stock will fade. For some years it was thought that SP Eastman stock wouldn't fade, but time has shown that it does. Fuji stock is reported to be low-fade stock, but only time will tell.

Selecting a quality movie projector to use in displaying your films is mostly a matter of taste and budget. Since projectors have been around for a long time, there are almost as many different types, models, and manufacturers as there are film collectors, and each person has a favorite machine. Here are a few of the manufacturers of 16mm projectors currently used by movie collectors: RCA, Graflex, Singer, Eiki, and Bell and Howell. Not all of these products are still manufactured today. Each company has its own requirements for projector lamps (bulbs), lenses, speakers, and other parts.

The same wide variety is available for standard 8mm and Super8 machines. Manufacturers of choice include Elmo and Eumig.

The films themselves can be purchased on reels or on cores. Cores are plastic plugs set in the center of a roll of film that are used to keep the film in a tight configuration for shipping without the need for heavy reels. Film on a core cannot be shown on a projector until the film has been transferred to a reel. Metal reels are preferred over plastic reels because plastic reels tend to squeak as film passes through them.

# An Overview of Film Values

This book is not intended for use as a price guide; however, the following chart of 1991 sample prices offers a general overview of mint condition film and cartoon values:

## 35mm Feature Films

| | |
|---|---|
| *Clash of the Titans* (1981) | $425 |
| *Crawling Hand* (1963) | 185 |
| *Five Card Stud* (1968), IB Tech | 350 |
| *Li'l Abner* (1959), IB Tech | 700 |
| *Spellbound* (1945), A. Hitchcock | 1500 |

## 16mm Feature Films

| | |
|---|---|
| *2001: A Space Odyssey* (1968) | $300 |
| *Adventures of Don Juan* (1948), E. Flynn | 600 |
| *African Queen* (1951), H. Bogart, IB Tech | 450 |
| *April Fools* (1969) | 50 |
| *Casablanca* (1941), H. Bogart | 400 |
| *Creature with the Atom Brain* (1955) | 175 |
| *Hell's Angels* (1930) | 300 |
| *Man from the Diner's Club* (1963) | 110 |
| *Man Who Knew Too Much* (1934), A. Hitchcock | 575 |
| *Penny Serenade* (1941), C. Grant | 250 |
| *Phantom of the Opera* (1925) | 575 |
| *Phantom of the Opera* (1943) | 425 |
| *Shane* (1953), IB Tech | 2000 |
| *Sunshine Boys* (1975) | 150 |
| *Tender Mercies* (1983) | 60 |
| *This Island Earth* (1954), IB Tech | 1000 |
| *Thunderball* (1965), IB Tech | 1500 |
| *Zorro the Gay Blade* (1981) | 60 |

## 16mm Cartoons

| | |
|---|---|
| "Betty Boop S.O.S." (1933) | $25 |
| "Felix and the Goose" (1936) | 50 |
| "Olive's Sweepstakes Ticket" (1941), Popeye | 35 |
| "Jungle Fool" (1929), Aesop's Fable | 35 |
| "Apes of Wrath" (1959), Bugs Bunny | 65 |
| "Daffy and the Dinosaur" (1939) | 65 |

## 8mm Feature Films

| | |
|---|---|
| *Wizard of Oz* (1939) | $100 |
| *Shall We Dance* (1937), F. Astaire, G. Rogers | 100 |
| *Murder by Decree* (1979), Sherlock Holmes | 100 |
| *Island of Dr. Moreau* (1977) | 75 |

# Sound on Film

Running along the side of a film strip is a recording of the sound that accompanies the film's images. The soundtrack may be either magnetic or optical. In the magnetic type, a strip of magnetic recording tape runs along the film's edge; in projection, the film's track is read by a sound head similar to that on a tape recorder. An optical soundtrack encodes sonic information in the form of patches of light and dark in a parallel line running alongside the frames. During production, electrical impulses from a microphone are translated into pulsations of light which are photographically inscribed on the moving film strip. When the film is projected, the optical track produces varying intensities of light which are translated back into electrical impulses and then into sound waves.

# Taking Care of Your Film Collection

Film will dry out over time and will become brittle and susceptible to sprocket damage. Dry film will not slide through the projector gate properly and can become permanently scratched. So keep your films in cans, sealed as completely as possible. To put moisture and limberness back into your prints, you should use a commercial solution like Surfaceset (from Filmagic Products, Inc., 204 14th St. N.W., P.O. Box 93584, Atlanta, GA 30318). This fluid cleans and preserves both acetate and vinyl films, and it works well on phonograph records and transparencies, too. You should treat your films at least once every three years.

You should store your films stacked flat on a shelf, rather than standing up on edge. With 16mm film there can be as much as 2,300 feet of film on each film reel. This represents an awful lot of weight hanging down on the sides of a reel of film. Over time, this weight can cause films stored upright on edge to stretch, scratch, and warp. For films stacked flat, the reel—rather than the film—will support the weight.

Metal cans are thought to contain fewer oxides and fumes than plastic cans, so opt for metal when possible. Keep film stored at 60 to 70°F in normal humidity. If the storage area is too dry, your film will dry out; if it is too wet, mildew may grow on your films. A good rule of thumb is that if you're comfortable, your film will be, too.

# Taking Care of Your Projector

Keep your projector away from dirt and dust and damp places, which can cause internal parts to rust. It only takes a minute to clean the gate of a projector with a soft-hair brush or can of air before running a film; it only takes a second for a small bit of dirt in the projector's film gate to scratch your film forever.

When you buy a used film, you should first run it through a rewinder, not a projector, using a soft cotton cloth or photowipes. (Photowipes—made of a dustless, lintless fabric and manufactured by Sorge Paper Co. of Middleton, Ohio—are available from most camera shops.) If you find a bad splice or broken sprocket and the film is printed on Mylar stock, you can resplice the film with tape. (You can easily determine if your film is Mylar by holding the reel up to the light. If you can see the shadow of your hand through the bulk of the film, the film is Mylar.) Do not use cement splices on Mylar, since the cement will break down the Mylar base of your film. If your damaged film is based on celluloid, you can safely resplice with either tape or cement.

If there is sprocket damage to only a few frames of your film, you can put a tape splice over the frames. Tape splices have their own punched-out sprocket holes to make up for the damaged sprockets. If you have a long section of sprocket damage, you can use a sprocket hole repair kit to lay a long strip of tape over the damaged area. A good sprocket hole repair kit, called Film-fix, is available from Marty Bahn and Co., 1974 N.E. 149th St., No. Miami, FL 33181.

# How to Buy Films

Outside of person-to-person exchanges of films at movie conventions, there is really only one way to buy prints of old movies: collector newspaper ads.

When buying films by mail through collector newspaper ads, you need to know more than just the title and the price of the movie being offered for sale. Since it's possible to copy a color film onto black-and-white film stock, you'll need to find out if the print of a color film is on color stock. You need to know the condition of the film, and, if it *is* a color print, you need to know the condition of the color—for example, is it good rich color, or has the print turned "red as a beet"?

The best way to answer all these questions is to pick up the phone and call the seller from the number given in the ad. (No phone number provided in an ad means no questions asked, and if you can't ask questions about a film you shouldn't buy it.) You can also use the call to verify if the print is still available (someone else might have already bought it), and if you decide to go ahead you can ask the seller to hold the print for you until your payment arrives.

Asking about the condition of a print is not an imposition. Sellers should have no hesitancy about telling you if the print is complete. Films edited for television and airlines exist with portions of the movie edited out; these edited prints are naturally less prized than the original full-length features. If the film in question was originally produced in Cinemascope, you'll want to ask if the print offered for sale is in "'scope'' or flat. A flat print of a 'scope print might not show all of each frame's image. A 'scope print projected without a 'scope lense on your projector will appear vertically squeezed.

If the film is older than, say, 1955, you should ask if the print is an original or a dupe. Many prints of popular titles are copies from copies, and the quality of the image can suffer from the copying process. If you're willing to buy a dupe of film—because you feel that you've got to have it now or that something better won't come along later—expect that the sound quality will drop along with the picture quality.

If you are considering a color film, ask what kind of stock the movie is printed on. If it's an older film, from before 1950, it might be printed on IB Tech stock. In this case, the color will not fade. If it's printed on any other stock, you should ask the seller about the quality of the color (as mentioned previously, color film stock fades over the years).

Another question you should ask concerns the seller's return policy. If you're not happy with the print, can you return it? If the seller says no, *beware*. Also find out about forms of payment accepted by the seller. Some dealers want cashier's checks or money orders in payment for their films, while other dealers will accept a personal check, after it has cleared at their bank.

After your film arrives you'll want to check it thoroughly for missing sections, heavy splicing, and visual quality. Assuming it is a color print, you also will want to check the Eastman stock code to get a feel for how long the color will stay good.

Film collecting is on the wane. The prices of the most sought-after titles will go up because the basic demand will be about level while the supply goes down as manufacturers of prints go out of business. The prices on less popular titles will go down because fewer and fewer people will seek them for collections.

# Collecting Videotapes

The major reason film prices are shifting is the increased interest in collecting videotapes for use at home. Today, in the comfort of your own easy chair, you can easily see the movie of your choice at the time of your choice on your videocassette recorder (VCR). This is good news, since many new release films never open locally in various parts of the country. For example, Academy Award winner *My Left Foot* (1989) played for only one week in my hometown at only one theater, but I can now rent or purchase a videotape copy and see the film at my leisure. That kind of convenience is almost impossible to resist.

Renting cassettes is the only way most people have of seeing innovative films, sleeper films, and foreign films. There are currently over 50 million VCR owners in America and a great number of mail-order video rental organizations, not to mention the thousands of suburban rental stores. This wealth of material coupled with other new forthcoming technological advancements promises that the ranks of film fans will swell beyond compare in the years to come.

One promising technological source for movie viewing enhancement is the laser disc. Laser-beam technology for music on compact discs was discussed in Chapter 7 of this book. The same basic technology is used for laser discs that provide a picture said to be 60 percent better than any current videocassette tape system. The sound, of course, is CD quality.

The laser disc gives you full surround sound. With speakers set behind you, you can experience true Dolby stereo and true separation. Anyone who owns a big-screen television and has it hooked up to a VCR is cheating himself or herself by not taking advantage of the high resolution results of a laser disc player. Visually speaking, videodiscs have cassettes beat every day of the week. The reason is that cassette tapes have only 260 lines of horizontal resolution, while discs have almost 360 lines. This constitutes a more than 25 percent increase in picture clarity. In fact, the quality of most laser discs approaches the best 16mm film prints.

The laser disc machine is a compact flat box a little smaller than most VCRs. It has a tray that slides out to receive a rainbow-hued silver videodisc. The tray with its lightweight cargo slides noiselessly back into the player, and because the laser beam reads the disc without touching it you can get countless perfect-quality plays from a virtually indestructible medium.

There are currently about 3,000 movies available on videodisc, as compared to 15,000 on VHS cassette. Disc prices range from $19.95 to $124.95 and are on the way down. Unlike tapes, discs offer immediate access to any point in a movie without the tiresome rewinding process. A laser disc player will not record off the air, but you can record from a laser disc to a videocassette and end up with a videocassette copy that is of broadcast quality.

The net result of all this technology is that you can own and collect more movies than ever before. Collecting films and videos gives you a library of Hollywood memorabilia that can provide a lifetime of thrills and enjoyment.

# CHAPTER 9

# Toys, Games, and Tie-ins

**B**Y FAR THE MOST POPULAR FORM OF MOVIE COLLECTIBLE is the licensed-agreement item. Known as 3-D items, tie-ins, children's character items, and mint and boxed memorabilia, these items are usually produced by a nonmovie business which has signed an agreement with the owner of a copyright associated with a film. The agreement typically allows the business to design, market, and sell items containing the logo or other graphic representation of a film or film character or personality.

What we're really talking about here is the flood of merchandise that is tied to a major motion picture, usually available right before and immediately after a film's release date. As an example of the astounding array of items available associated with a single film, here's a partial list of items that were connected to the release of *Batman* (1989):

Boys' and mens' woven shirts
Sweatshirts
T-shirts
Sunglasses and visors
Shoes
Suspenders
Pantyhose
Cloisonné pins, earrings, and key chains
Pajamas and robes
Wristwatches
Cosmetic bags
Umbrellas
Jogging suits
Sneakers
Unpainted diecast figures

Battery- and pedal-powered ride-in
    Batmobiles
Latex masks
Cassette storybooks
Colorform activity sets
Paint-by-number sets
Remote-control batcopters
Handmade electric guitars
Sleeping bags, bedspreads, and
    pillowcases
Beach and bath towels
Alarm clocks
Adhesive bandages
Cake pans and cookie cutters
Auto seat covers

Fig. 9-1. Movie-related toys and models. Left to right: talking Robby the Robot, Audrey II bank, Aurora's Phantom of the Opera model, plaster replica of the Maltese Falcon.

Balloons
Computer software games
Tricycles, bikes, and scooters
Yoyos
Kites
Skateboards
Paddle balls
Silly Putty
Walkie-talkies
Articulated figures
Pinball games
Batarangs
Ice skates

Gold and silver necklaces
Bookends
Credit card wallets
Bumper stickers
Hand puppets
Christmas ornaments
Auto air fresheners
Candy and candy dispensers
Thimbles
Auto sunshades
Gum with trading cards
Jigsaw puzzles
Compact discs
Postcards and greeting cards

**Fig. 9-2.** Charlie Chaplin doll with molded composition head and straw-filled body. Louis Amberg & Son first made this doll in 1915; the company's trademark is found on the left sleeve of the doll's coat.

It has been said that *Batman* made more money at the merchandising counter than at the box office. This may not be exactly true, but at least all that "free advertising" helped draw interest to the film and probably paid for the movie's basic advertising program as well. No doubt about it—movie merchandise is big business.

There are three types of collectors for this type of movie memorabilia. Many collectors are content to acquire nonworking examples of toys for display purposes only. Prices for these items are quite reasonable, depending on condition and rarity. Other collectors want their items (for example, wristwatches) to work so they can wind them up and wear them—or whatever. Finally, a few collectors seek only pristine, unused, "mint condition in the original box" items. Because such items are so rare and demand for them is so intense, these items end up selling for record-breaking prices at auctions.

The next several pages provide discussions of the major collecting categories for licensed movie memorabilia.

Fig. 9-3. Decca records offered this record duster featuring Bing Crosby as an advertising giveaway for stores that carried its products. (Like many movie personalities, Crosby enjoyed a multifaceted career.)

# School Supplies

The most popular type of movie-related school supplies collected today is the lunch box and thermos set designed with illustrations from films like *101 Dalmations* (1961) and *Planet of the Apes* (1968). The old, mini-billboard graphic design on the rectangular lunch box is an image from the childhood years of many collectors. The current trend is to separate the lunch box from its thermos, but this seems a bit unfair since the items were originally sold as a set. The standard size of a lunch box is 7″ × 4″ × 8 1/2″; the thermos is approximately 6 1/2″ tall.

Other school supplies manufactured to allow children to take reminders of their favorite movies into the study hall are pencils, rulers, folders, pencil sharpeners, paint boxes, and ruled tablets with colored covers. The recent youth interest in stickers for decorative and trading purposes has also found a successful niche in schoolrooms. All of these items are collectible as movie memorabilia.

# Toys

As you can imagine, over the last hundred years there have been thousands of types of movie-related toys manufactured. Like many other types of movie memorabilia, the category of toys is a collectible category unto itself. It is a large and varied category; for discussion here, the materials used to construct toys provides a reasonable beginning for sorting out the many types of toys.

There are cast-iron, tin, and celluloid toys popular from the turn of the century to the mid-1950s. There are plastic, vinyl, and rubber toys available from post-World War II technology. Wooden figures and plush dolls are basic toys made from basic materials.

Almost any toy is considered more valuable if it is preserved in its original box. Even the empty boxes from plastic model kits of movie characters such as Frankenstein or The Phantom of the Opera have a high value in today's toy market. (Noted toy model manufacturers are Monogram, Aurora, and Winslow.)

Much of the list of Batman items presented earlier in this chapter are part of the toy category, and for every item listed, you can expect to find one that isn't. That's how diverse and wide-ranging this category is. Obviously, any type of toy can be imprinted with a logo and marketed as a licensed ''official'' item associated with a film. This means that timing is perhaps the most important aspect of any sale of movie-related toys.

An auction or convention assembles the widest selection of buyers for toys. For example, a science fiction convention is a likely place to sell an articulating figure doll of Mr. Spock from *Star Trek: The Motion Picture* (1979), and a B-movie convention that focuses on Westerns is the perfect place to buy or sell a Hopalong Cassidy cap pistol.

In the 1930s, parents and grandparents could give children toys associated with Hollywood personalities. These included Harold Lloyd sparkler toys, Charlie Chaplin windup toys, Shirley Temple dolls, Our Gang boxed puzzles, and Douglas Fairbanks cardboard masks. As the years rolled on, wave after wave of coloring books, paper dolls, and other movie-related toys washed over the country, delighting children of all ages. A few more examples: board games like ''Movie Millions: The Glamorous Game'' (1938), wherein each player tries to complete production on a motion picture before his or her opponents; Bugs Bunny soft rubber squeaker toys; Popeye paint and crayon set; James Bond Aston-Martin toy car complete with ejection seat.

The toy category includes some fairly common larger items, such as bicycles sporting movie- or cartoon-related features (for example, Gene Autry's saddlebags or Donald Duck's face). Wrist and pocket watches sporting these kinds of features can also be included in the toy collectibles category. (Incredibly enough, in 1990 a Mickey Mouse pocket watch with a metal fob sold for over $3,000.)

The recent rapid rise in the prices of old toys has caused moaning and groaning among some collectors because they see their chances of ever acquiring certain toys at affordable prices becoming slimmer and slimmer. On the other hand, other collectors relish the thought that at last movie-related toys have earned an important place among collectibles; these collectors count themselves among those fortunate enough to have bought when prices were relatively low. The truth is—and we all knew it from the beginning—that whoever is willing to spend the most money will die with the most toys.

**Fig. 9-4.** In 1926 Milton Bradley issued several "Movie-Land Puzzle" sets, each of which featured two scenes from a movie of that era; this one combined an *Our Gang* scene from a Pathe Comedy with a scene from De Mille Production's *The Yankee Clipper*.

**Fig. 9-5.** Wilder Manufacturing Company's 1930 "Movie-Land Cut Ups" three-puzzle set included a scene featuring Harry Langdon. These die-cut cardboard puzzles of the late 1920s set the stage for the great jigsaw puzzle craze of 1932–33.

Fig. 9-6. McCormick's "Elvis #2" whiskey bottle with a music box, issued in 1979. The image of Elvis appears in hundreds of collectible forms, not the least of which is a series of limited edition whiskey bottles.

# Dolls and Figurines

Paper dolls and articulating dolls have already been mentioned, but there are many other types within this category that are highly collectible. For example, china and bisque dolls are highly prized. Most china dolls have a body made of stuffed cloth with a fragile china head and china hands attached.

One of the most interesting stories related to movie memorabilia dolls involves Disney's Mickey Mouse. In the early 1930s a woman named Charlotte Clark produced a series of handmade stuffed Mickey and Minnie dolls, which Walt Disney is said to have loved. In addition to the actual doll designs, Clark created a series of patterns for distribution by the McCall Company so that aunts and grandmothers across the country could fabricate individual Mickey Mouse designs. As recently as the 1950s, it was possible to purchase a pattern and make a charming version of Mickey the cowboy or Mickey the pirate.

Figurines range in size from 2″ to 20″. Made of porcelain or plaster, these decorative items are displayed on shelves or in china hutches, adding a bit of Hollywood to dining

**Fig. 9-7.** Betty Boop beechwood ukulele with red celluloid fingerboard and yellow ground body upon which are red, blue, and green illustrations of Betty, Ko Ko, and Bimbo.

Fig. 9-8. The Fanny Brice "Baby Snooks" doll manufactured by Ideal. The doll has composition head, hands, and feet, and its body flexes due to a wire construction.

rooms and parlors. A set of four Marx Brothers bisque figures from the 1930s can brighten up any room. The popularity of figurines encouraged manufacturers to produce novelties such as beer mugs in the shape of W. C. Fields and electric lamps built from figures of Roy Rogers riding Trigger.

Traditionally, the largest share of movie tie-in items came from four categories: Disneyana, space adventure (for example, *Star Trek* and *Star Wars*), pinup art, and Western heroes.

# Disneyana

Disneyana is the largest, most popular subcategory of toys related to movie memorabilia. After Walt Disney lost control of his Oswald Rabbit character to distributor M. J. Winkler's estate, Walt realized the importance of owning and controlling copyrights to the characters he created. This lesson was firmly in place when Mickey Mouse was introduced in the late 1920s. Since that time, literally thousands of Disney items have been licensed for both the series characters (like Mickey and Donald) and the feature characters (like Cinderella and Peter Pan). Today's *Ducktales* (1990) is only the latest in a long line of Disney movies that have generated tons of Disneyana.

By and large, Disneyana is marked "Walt Disney Productions" after September 1938, when the basic licensing agreements were rewritten by Walt's attorneys, and initialed "WDP" after 1939. It's also possible to find items marked "Walt Disney Enterprises." Over the years, Mickey and Donald have changed in outward appearance, and so have their memorabilia. Mickey once had large black dots for eyes with "pie slice" white triangles to represent their glow. And he always sported a long thin tail. In later years, animators grew tired of drawing the wiry tail in every frame of a cartoon, so it was dropped. And Mickey's eyes gained comma-shaped eyebrows to add expression to the character's face. Donald changed from a long-necked, pointed-beak waddler to the more rounded and natural figure he is today.

Disneyana has been applied to nearly every conceivable product in the last six decades with no end in sight. A set of child's chamber pot bowls of porcelain-clad metal with color illustrations of Mickey and Minnie are said to have been autographed and given as baby gifts by Walt Disney. An Emerson Electric radio encased in a sculpted and painted wooden housing featuring Snow White and the Seven Dwarfs is a highly sought-after item today. So are Mickey Mouse toothbrush holders and Donald Duck soda pop. Disneyana can be found in such diverse forms as pez dispensers, cookie jars, nightlights, dart boards, bubble gum cards, halloween costumes, greeting cards, and nursery decorations, to name a few.

# Space Adventure

An interest in space adventures has been associated with the movies since George Melies's special effects short subject *A Trip to the Moon* (1902) and Fritz Lang's *Girl in the Moon* (1929). Hardly a boy or girl in America during the 1930s didn't attend with enthusiasm the Buck Rogers and Flash Gordon serials starring Buster Crabbe. In the 1950s, the UFO scare and the launching of the USSR sputnik encouraged producers to fill the silver screen with all sorts of saucermen, star creatures, and invaders from Mars. The space program of the 1960s popularized NASA and "serious" space exploration. On television we were introduced to the characters of the television show "Star Trek," who later boldly went to the big screen in a series of successful motion pictures. And, of course, there is the recent, hugely popular epic of *Star Wars*.

The attraction for tie-ins to space adventure movies is almost as fantastic as the films themselves. There are *Star Trek* fan clubs in operation within almost every state of the union. For nearly 20 years, annual *Star Trek* conventions have taken place across the country. With each new film, the legion of "trekkies" expands. Major stars of the movies and the new television program appear before interested fans, in between other convention events like costume contests, blooper reels, Star Fleet business meetings, and a dealers room stocked with virtually every known type of *Star Trek* memorabilia.

In fact, there is so much *Star Trek* material around that serious collectors have difficulty sorting out authentic, original props (phasers, uniforms, pointy Spock ears, and so on) from convincing but unauthorized duplicates. And make no mistake, original props are available. For example, even though there was tight security on the set during the filming of *The Wrath of Khan* (1982), several original props were stolen. In addition, some of the props were sold to charity auctions by performers and members of the film crew. At one such event, a set of Mr. Spock's ears went for over $1,000. Other unusual *Star Trek* items include a set of four Dr. Pepper drinking glasses, Proctor and Gamble commemorative posters, and the original arcade game by Sega valued at over $2,000.

The excitement generated by George Lucas' *Star Wars* films is almost as intoxicating as that generated by Gene Roddenberry's *Star Trek*. Lucas does not support *Star Wars* conventions or fan clubs, but each year new rumors circulate that more films in the series soon will begin production. The studios know that movies about the Clone Wars and Jedi Knights are sure moneymakers, so it's only a matter of time before Lucas decides to give the go-ahead for more adventures of C3PO and R2-D2. Meanwhile, space adventure film fans wait in eager anticipation.

The anticipation for the second *Star Wars* movie, *Return of the Jedi* (1983), was so great that it created a cluster of rare collectible items. These items were already in production when the film's title was changed. Originally titled *Revenge of the Jedi* (not unlike the previous year's *Star Trek* adventure *The Wrath of Khan*), the film had been promoted to an eager and hungry audience of fans and merchandisers, causing many collectibles (both authorized and unauthorized) to be placed in the market with the wrong movie title attached. It may seem like a minor point, but it's not minor to true *Star Wars* fans who might consider it an absolute necessity to own items with both imprints.

Unusual *Star Wars* items include a Kenner radio-controlled R2-D2, *Star Wars* party hats and plates, and the Parker Brothers video arcade game that sells for over $1,000.

# Pinup Art

There has always been a strong sensual side to movies—glamour queens, sex goddesses, and hunks of beefcake have always ruled the screen. Through the years, the likes of Rudolph Valentino, Mae West, Betty Grable, Marilyn Monroe, and Marylin Chambers have made the blood boil and the heart beat faster.

Many a movie poster or advertisement has relied on the old adage "Sex sells." Think of Jane Russell in *The Outlaw* (1943) or Raquel Welch in *One Million Years B.C.* (1966) and you'll realize how film has provided sensual images for generations of film fans. Key to this type of collectible are giveaway pinups by such entertaining artists as Earl Morgan, Varga, Petty, and Bradshaw Crandall. Whether the illustrations of film stars like Barbara Stanwyck or Ava Gardner are on calendars or playing cards, the message is clear: pinups are popular and Hollywood pinups are highly popular.

# Western Heroes

If you live west of the Mississippi River, you live in "The West," and you probably have seen more westerns than have film fans living east of the "Mighty Mississip." This doesn't mean that cowboy stars like Lash LaRue, Roy Rogers, and Bob Steele don't have fans in Pennsylvania and North Carolina; they do. But it's just a fact of life and geography that there are more western fans in the West than in the East.

Generations of boys and girls experienced B Westerns via Saturday matinees and afternoon television. Thousands of short (approximately 60 minutes each) black-and-white features and double features still flicker across screens from St. Louis to San Diego, week in and week out. This is the idealized West where "men are men and women are glad of it." Black hats and quick draws from the hip. Wonderful stuff surrounding the likes of Buck Jones, Don "Red" Barry, Hopalong Cassidy, Bob Allen, Rex Bell, Bill Elliott, Eddie Dean, Tim Holt, Monte Hale, Kermit Maynard, Johnny Mack Brown, Charles Starrett, Col. Tim McCoy, Ken Maynard, Tom Tyler, Jimmy Wakely, Allen "Rocky" Lane, Tex Ritter, Tom Keene, Gene Autry, Whip Wilson, Sunset Carson, Big Boy Williams, Hoot Gibson, and an hombre named Marion Morrison (John Wayne). Each of these good ol' boy owlhoots made dozens of B Westerns throughout the 1930s and 1940s. And even today, their fans are a fighting legion.

For each successful cowboy film star there were also dozens of tie-ins and toys for the youngun's to yearn for, creating western movie memorabilia like the Buck Jones "Ranger-Cowboy" song manual, Red Ryder 78 rpm records, the Tom Mix souvenir bandanna, the Gene Autry guitar, the Lone Ranger hairbrush, the Roy Rogers bedspread, and the Tim McCoy Big Little Book.

The annual Tom Mix Festival honoring the late movie cowboy matinee idol of the silver screen is an example of how the western hero will never be forgotten. Several of Tom Mix's grandchildren attend the event, plus fans from the United States, Canada, Mexico, and Europe. In the 1930s, the Ralston Purina Company established a national fan club called the Tom Mix Ralston Straight Shooters to which millions of boys and girls belonged. Tom Mix was a crossover star, appearing both in films and on the radio. His adventures also appeared in several series of comic books, the most recent of which appeared in 1990 from the American Comic Company.

One of the hottest collectibles in recent years is the movie-related toy model kit. Manufactured by the Aurora Model Kit Company beginning in the mid-1960s to bolster the company's floundering airplane and automobile model kit business, these scary, plastic multipart models were assembled, glued, painted, and built into elaborate scenes commemorating the horror films shown on late night Chiller Theatres. Today, the Japanese have led a revival of interest in these little plastic creatures, fabricating new variations of old monsters and totally new models of current creatures like *Alien* and *Predator*.

More than the collectibles in any other category, toys, tie-ins, and 3-D items are targeted for the juvenile movie audience—and those who want to "return to those thrilling days of yesteryear" to recapture the yesteryear of youth. Movies convincingly take us to places we've never been or to fantasy places we haven't "seen" in years. They let us visit never-never land ... the land beyond beyond ... long, long ago, in a galaxy far away ... back to the future ... somewhere over the rainbow.

# CHAPTER 10

# Autographs, Costumes, Animation Cels, and Novelties

I DOUBT THAT IT'S POSSIBLE TO RECORD every type of movie memorabilia ever created. The influence of the film industry has been so strong throughout our culture that literally every sort of popular product has been associated, at one time or other, with some aspect of moviemaking or movie viewing. Most other types of collectibles, such as comic books, autographs, photographs, and toys, have movie star and movie character subcategories.

Advertising has connected hundreds of movie stars with thousands of products; everything from cars to toothpaste has been promoted by famous Hollywood film stars. The point is that you never know when or where you'll discover some new "gem" of movie memorabilia. It's all around us, easily accessible and fun to collect.

## Autographs

Many people collect autographs of sports stars, politicians, and musicians, but the largest portion of the overall autograph hobby involves the collecting of movie star autographs. This is another indication of the comprehensive influence movies have on the American consciousness.

Autograph hunting was once an innocent occupation, chiefly for young people, that involved hanging around outside a studio, a theater, a restaurant, or a nightspot in the hope of obtaining the autograph of a prominent personality. Today, autographs have become big business.

Many of the factors that influence the value of a celebrity's autograph are related to supply and demand. Greta Garbo's signature is particularly elusive, making it valuable to the tune of $15,000. A letter that is handwritten, as opposed to typewritten, can often be more valuable than an autographed photograph or greeting card. The contents of the letter can raise the value of the autograph considerably, if they add insight into the signer's

Fig. 10-1 An inscribed autograph on a dated first-day issue postcard. Alan Alda's signature is rare (the star is known to sign only for special causes or friends).

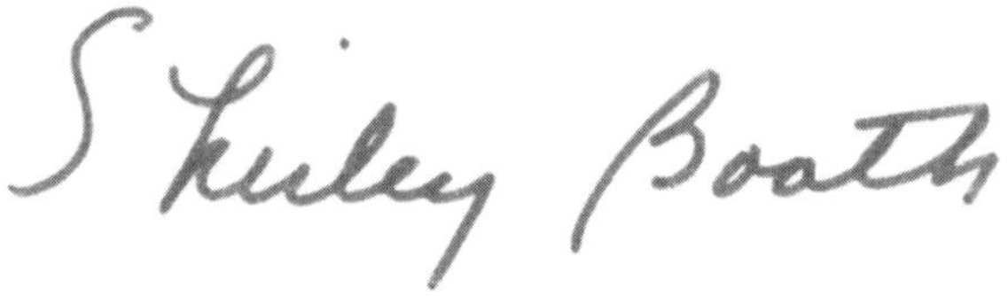

Fig. 10-2. Shirley Booth autograph on 3″ × 5″ card.

Fig. 10-3. Signature card of Rod Steiger.

**Fig. 10-4.** Autograph and movie fan Keith Hurd posed with film star Linnea Quigley at a movie convention; then, months later, Hurd had the photo with him when he again met the actress, and he asked her to add her signature to the photo.

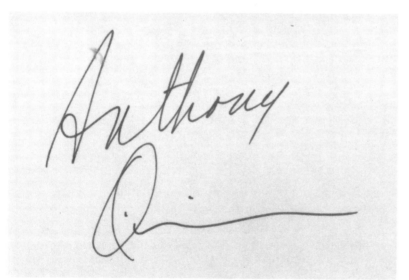

**Fig. 10-5.** Signature card of Anthony Quinn.

**Fig. 10-6.** Photo of TV star Ricky Schroder printed with signature as part of the graphic element (not a true autograph).

life and career. A signature on a legal document is valued more than a signed photo because there is little or no question of the signature's authenticity. A signed check or credit card receipt is valuable for the same reason.

A celebrity's signature is sometimes the most difficult collectible to authenticate. A dealer in autographs will often issue a certificate of authenticity to the buyer of an autograph and will usually offer to refund the purchase price if the autograph should prove to be a fake.

One of the major problems in the autograph collecting field is that some famous signatures have been produced via an Autopen or Signa-Signer. Such a device creates handwriting that is almost indistinguishable from the real thing—except that there are no pressure points in the signature and each signature is *exactly* the same as all the others. The problem of authenticity is further clouded by the "autographs" that are created by rubber stamps, secretaries, and fan mail services.

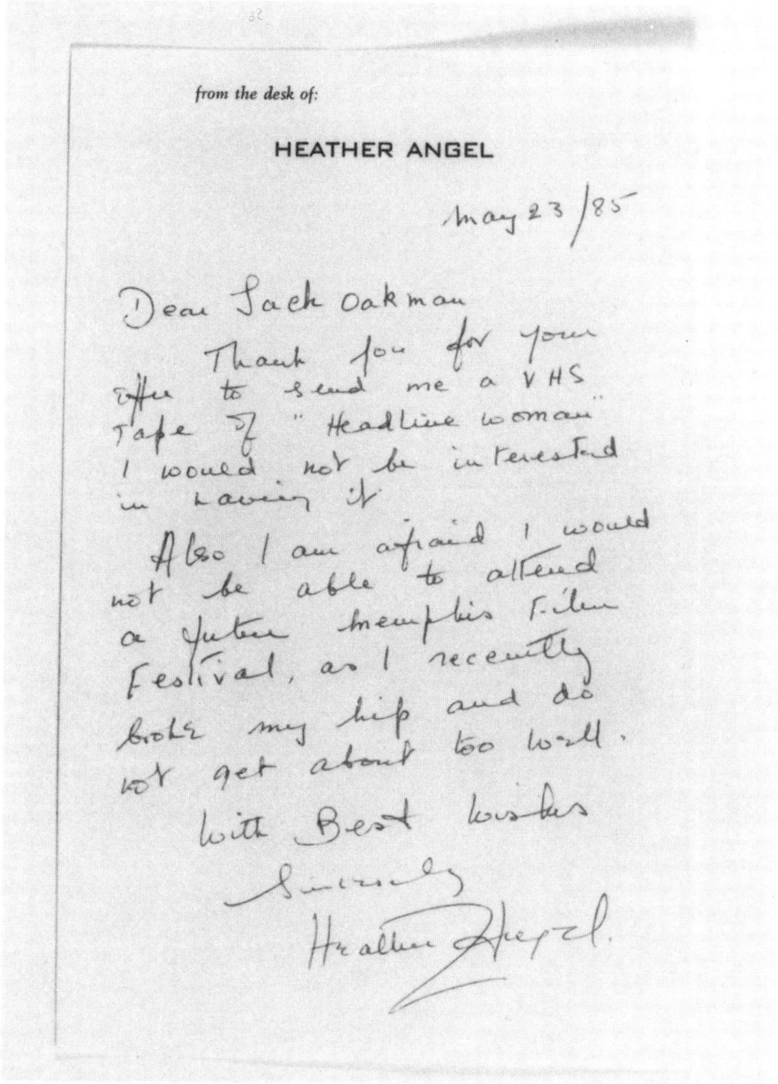

from the desk of:

**HEATHER ANGEL**

may 23/85

Dear Jack Oakman

Thank you for your offer to send me a VHS Tape of "Headline woman" I would not be interested in having it

Also I am afraid I would not be able to attend a future memphis Film Festival, as I recently broke my hip and do not get about too well.

With Best wishes

Sincerely

Heather Angel.

Fig. 10-7. Handwritten letter with signature of Heather Angel.

There are many things to be aware of if you decide to collect autographs. Some fan photographs are printed with signatures on the negative so the "autograph" is printed and developed at the same time as the photo (see Fig. 10-6). And Hollywood studios of the 1930s and 1940s hired office workers to sit all day doing nothing except responding to—and "signing" their response to—movie star fan mail.

Quite often a signature will change style over the years. If possible, you might want to collect samples of autographs from the early, middle, and late years of a star's popularity. Earlier signatures are the more valuable.

These various problems are not insurmountable, and you should, after some practice,

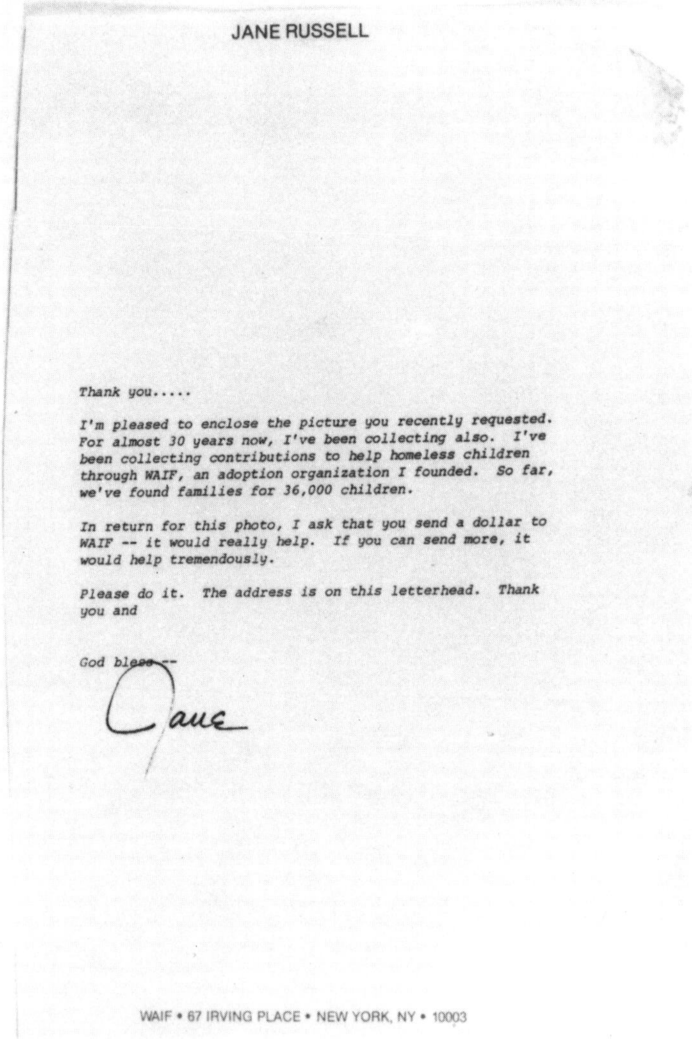

**JANE RUSSELL**

Thank you.....

I'm pleased to enclose the picture you recently requested.
For almost 30 years now, I've been collecting also. I've
been collecting contributions to help homeless children
through WAIF, an adoption organization I founded. So far,
we've found families for 36,000 children.

In return for this photo, I ask that you send a dollar to
WAIF -- it would really help. If you can send more, it
would help tremendously.

Please do it. The address is on this letterhead. Thank
you and

God bless --

*Jane*

WAIF • 67 IRVING PLACE • NEW YORK, NY • 10003

**Fig. 10-8.** Typed letter with first name signature of Jane Russell.

**Fig. 10-9.** Signature card of Barbara Stanwyck.

146

ENDORSEMENT OF THIS CHECK BY PAYEE ACKNOWLEDGES RECEIPT IN FULL FOR THE FOLLOWING ACCOUNTS

| DESCRIPTION | AMOUNT |
| --- | --- |
| Legal Retainer for 11/8 | 200 - |
| CHARGE — GROSS AMOUNT | |
| DISCOUNT | |
| AMOUNT PAYABLE | 200 - |

SPECIAL ACCOUNT
Cecil B. De Mille Productions, Inc.
2010 DeMille Drive
Hollywood, Calif.

Nº 4934

PAY TO THE ORDER OF

DATE Nov 11 1947

Neil S McCarthy $200.00

THE SUM DOLLARS

16-5 LOS ANGELES MAIN OFFICE 16-5
Bank of America
NATIONAL TRUST AND SAVINGS ASSOCIATION
660 South Spring Street
LOS ANGELES, CALIFORNIA

SPECIAL ACCOUNT
CECIL B. DeMILLE PRODUCTIONS, INC.
Cecil B. deMille
Secretary

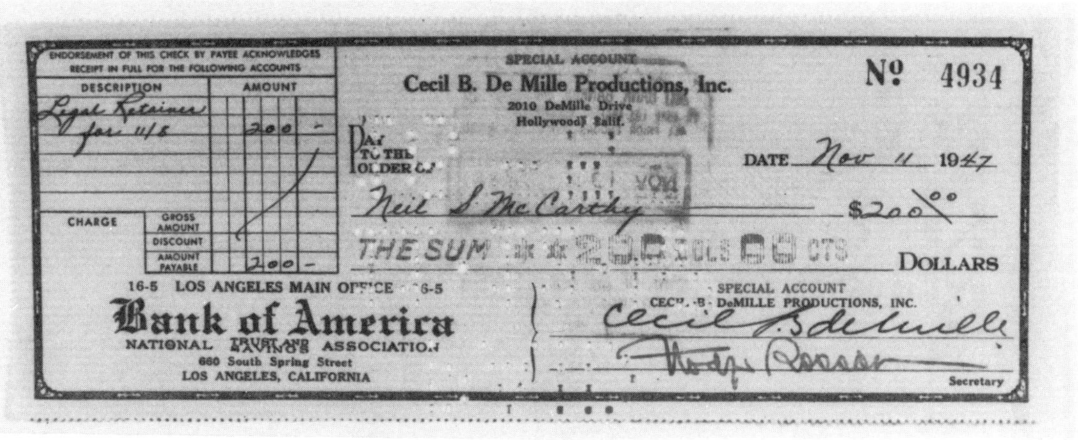

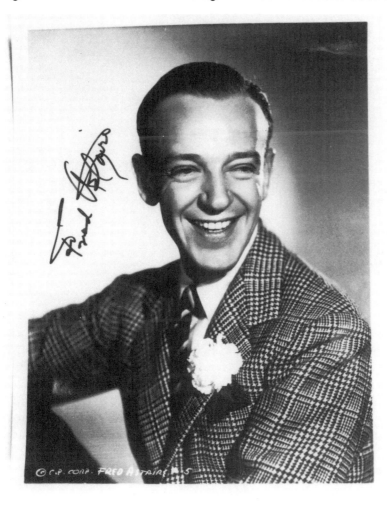

Fig. 10-10. Cancelled and countersigned check of director Cecil B. DeMille.

Fig. 10-11. Portrait photo of Fred Astaire with autograph.

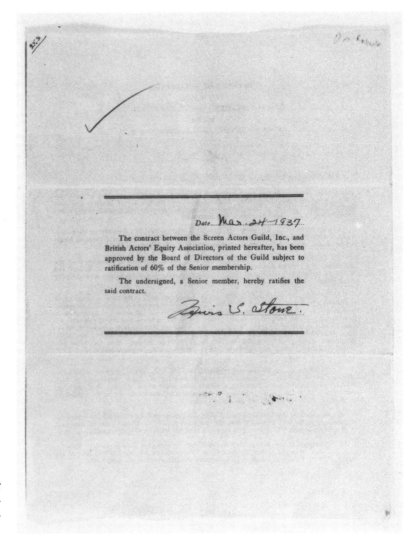

**Fig. 10-12.** Signed contract of March 24, 1937, containing actor Lewis Stone's signature.

be able to authenticate most of your movie star collection. The good news is that autographs can be collected rather easily by mail or through dealers. A few extra minutes at a book signing or a regional theater performance can net you a treasured signature (and if you get a signature in person you know it is authentic). A letter mailed to a Hollywood star will almost always bring you back an autograph. Be sure to include return postage, and you might like to send along a photograph for signing or a 3″ × 5″ card. Signed photos are more sought after by other collectors, but 3″ × 5″ cards can be matted after the signing to a photo of your choice, creating an attractive display. Cards are more easily stored and collected into albums, too.

Fig. 10-13. Autographed still of Boris Karloff.

Here are three books you can use as sources of movie star addresses in order to send away for Hollywood autographs:

- *The Address Book* by Michael Levine, G. P. Putnam's Sons, 200 Madison Ave., New York, NY 10016
- *Earl Blackwell's Celebrity Register,* Gale Research, 1780 Broadway, New York, NY 10019
- *Christiansen's Ultimate TV, Movie and Rock and Roll Directory,* Cardiff-By-The-Sea, 6065 Mission Gorge Rd., San Diego, CA 92120

More good news is the fact that you should have little trouble finding autographs in attics and flea markets by carefully inspecting old books and bundles of letters and papers. This makes autograph collecting one of the least expensive and most fun ways of collecting rare items.

**Fig. 10-14.** Pinup photo signed by Janet Leigh.

Autograph values can be influenced by various factors—for example, whether the signature is in ink or pencil; whether it was signed at the height of a star's career or after retirement; and whether it is inscribed, say "To John", instead of just being a lone signature. To give you a general idea of the range of autograph values, a chart of sample 1991 autograph prices is provided below:

| | |
|---|---:|
| Woody Allen, signed portrait | $ 15 |
| Goldie Hawn, signed portrait | 18 |
| John Wayne, signed portrait | 75 |
| Sean Connery as 007, signed portrait | 18 |
| Errol Flynn, signed portrait | 200 |
| Greta Garbo, signed portrait | 4100 |

**Fig. 10-15.** Double signature of Fredric March and Claudette Colbert.

| | |
|---|---:|
| Alfred Hitchcock, signed portrait | $ 300 |
| Marilyn Monroe, signed portrait | 650 |
| Elvis Presley, signed portrait | 700 |
| Tony Curtis, Jack Lemmon, *Some Like It Hot,* portrait | 23 |
| Dustin Hoffman, Tom Cruise, *Rainman,* signed portrait | 25 |
| Ivonne Craig as Batgirl, signed portrait | 13 |
| Tom Selleck, signed portrait | 35 |
| James Stewart, photo matted with signed card | 60 |
| Marilyn Monroe, photo matted with signed portcard | 9900 |
| Walt Disney, photo matted with signed card | 600 |
| Lon Chaney Jr., photo matted with signed card | 200 |
| Roger Moore, photo matted with signed card | 40 |
| Eddie Cantor, photo matted with signed card | 75 |
| Lex Baxter, signature | 30 |
| James Cagney, signature | 35 |
| John Wayne, signature | 75 |
| Natalie Wood, signature | 30 |
| Gracie Allen, signature | 25 |
| Humphrey Bogart, signature | 175 |
| Bing Crosby, signature | 40 |
| Spencer Tracy, signature | 95 |
| Lewis Stone, signed contract | 25 |

**Fig. 10-16.** Multiple autographs of various RKO stars captured on a black-and-white still: George Montgomery, Joan Bennett, James Stewart, Jeff Morrow, Lyle Talbot, Marie Windsor, Ben Johnson, and more.

| | |
|---|---|
| Boris Karloff, signed contract | $1500 |
| Marilyn Monroe, signed check | 3300 |
| Charlie Chaplin, signed contract | 2200 |

Many autograph collectors specialize in a particular genre; for example, the collecting of signatures of Academy Award winners is quite popular. Serious collectors might like to join the Manuscript Society or the Universal Autograph Collectors Club, or at least do business with members of these two groups. Each group fosters an exchange of information and knowledge on the subject of autographs through regular meetings and newsletters. The addresses of these organizations are:

Universal Autograph Collectors Club
P.O. Box 467
Rockville Center, NY 11571

Manuscript Society
c/o David R. Smith, Exec. Director
350 N. Niagara St.
Burbank, CA 91505

# Costumes

Another popular item available at auctions and conventions is the clothing or costumes worn during the filming of a movie. Quite often a studio or celebrity will keep a garment worn in a film, eventually handing it over to museums for exhibition. Usually a studio label is sewn into the garment. Often, the star's name or the costume designer's name (for example, Edith Head, Walter Plunkett) will also appear on a label within the garment. Thus, collectors can be reasonably assured the costume is an original and was worn by the star the seller claims wore it.

Studio auctions are not very common, but auctions of the possessions of Hollywood personalities are becoming quite frequent. Bette Midler recently purchased a collection of Mary Pickford's costumes at an estate auction, as did the owner of one of the finest collections of Hollywood costumes: Debbie Reynolds. Even the most simple movie costumes are bringing high prices, and a few common items, such as a handbag used by Marilyn Monroe, fetch prices over $1,000.

Interest in motion-picture costumes has picked up dramatically in the last few years. Whereas other types of movie memorabilia like magazines and autographs are available in a specific form by the hundreds and thousands, costumes are usually one-of-a-kind creations, making them quite rare and special. Artist sketches of costumes before actual manufacture have also become hot collector's items. These sketches represent a more-conventional artistic level, similar to the drawings and paintings by famous American illustrators like Rockwell and Wyeth.

It's possible to attend conventions where a star is appearing and find that some of

**Fig. 10-17.** Costume worn by Tyrone Power in *The Mark of Zorro* (1940). This is a grey two-piece wool suit with the actor's name sewn inside collar.

the costumes worn by the star in the filming of a motion picture are available for sale or auction to the convention attendees. Striking up an acquaintance with a film personality has also proven to be a good way to ultimately acquire costumes, as well as other select items of movie memorabilia. However, you should be cautioned against pestering recognized Hollywood figures purely for the purpose of obtaining a bargain-priced piece of film history.

**Fig. 10-18.** Two pairs of matching shoes worn by Gene Kelly and Frank Sinatra in *Take Me Out to the Ball Game* (1949), custom-made of orchid leather and beige suede. The actors' names are inscribed inside.

As noted elsewhere, this book is not a price guide; however, it is interesting to take a look at some recent values for a variety of specific costumes:

| | |
|---|---|
| Suit worn by Elvis Presley in *It Happened at the World's Fair* | $2400 |
| Dress worn by Judy Garland in *The Wizard of Oz* | 4950 |
| Costume worn by Buddy Hackett in *The Wonderful World of the Brothers Grimm* | 300 |
| Three-piece suit worn by Gene Kelly in *Brigadoon* | 1000 |
| Robe worn by Norma Shearer in *Marie Antoinette* | 2750 |
| Suit worn by Clark Gable in *Gone With the Wind* | 8500 |
| Coat worn by Lana Turner in *The Bad and the Beautiful* | 350 |
| Dress worn by Linda Darnell in *Forever Amber* | 500 |
| Dress worn by Jack Lemmon in *Some Like It Hot* | 2000 |
| Pants worn by Robert Redford in *Butch Cassidy and the Sundance Kid* | 600 |
| Flight Suit worn by Keir Dullea in *2001: A Space Oddessy* | 1700 |

**Fig. 10-19.** Period robe worn by Norma Shearer in *Marie Antoinette* (1938). Designed by Adrian, this garment is made of steel-grey silk satin brocade trimmed with beige fur.

| | |
|---|---:|
| Shoes worn by Fred Astaire and Ginger Rogers in *The Gay Divorcee* | 9000 |
| Costume worn by Tyrone Power in *The Mark of Zorro* | 2250 |
| Swimsuit worn by Esther Williams in *Bathing Beauty* | 1100 |

Great care should be taken when collecting and handling costumes. The flexible nature of cloth and leather makes these materials fragile over time. When inspecting a prospective purchase from the dressing rooms of the golden age of Hollywood, always treat the garment as if it were made of spun gold or fairy dust. Perhaps, in a way, it is.

# Cels and Novelties

Animation cels are sheets of celluloid (or, in early examples, nitrate-based plastic) used in the production of animated cartoon shorts, full-length animated features, and any other purposes for which animation is used. Each cel becomes a frame in the film after being reduced photographically to 32mm or 64mm film.

Currently about 500 galleries nationwide specialize in the sale of animation items. Dealers who collected cels back when they were available from souvenir shops in Disneyland for as little as $1.50 each are definitely whistling while they work.

Cels were never supposed to be finished works of art. Each image was inked and painted on clear celluloid and designed to fill one frame of film. Twenty-four frames take up a second of screen time. A typical six- to eight-minute cartoon used more than 10,000 drawings (cels). Each cel was intended to last only long enough to get from the ink and paint department to the camera department.

For connoisseurs, the blue chips of the market are vintage prewar cels from such films as *Snow White* and *Pinocchio*. A particular prewar cel's individual value is based on quality and condition and on the significance of the scene it depicts. The vintage cels are quite valuable in general partly because the early artwork was so sophisticated and partly because so many cels are gone now. Some were washed clean and reused during World War II because petroleum products were vital to the war effort. Also, many Warner Brothers cels were said to have been destroyed in the 1960s to make room for storage.

Today, collectors also pay big bucks for so-called limited edition cels—cartoon work that has never been under a camera or projected on a screen. These copies of classic scenes (often complete with backgrounds) are much like the porcelain plates promoted in magazine and television ads, but they sell for $500 to $2,000!

Collectors who don't like the idea of "copy cels" need not despair, for a wide variety of originals are available. Cels range from "multi-cel setups" (several full or trimmed celluloids placed together to form a scene) and "full sheets" (the entire piece of plastic, often including the registration holes) down to "partial celluloids" (those with excess plastic cut away, sometimes right down to the black outline of the image).

Backgrounds are even more varied. Some were hand prepared (done by who knows whom, usually to make the cel attractive when framed). Others have production backgrounds (done by the actual studio, although not necessarily for the same film as the cel)

**Fig. 10-20.** Cel of Pongo and Lucky from *101 Dalmations* (1961). Cel is gouache on celluloid with lithographed background. (© Walt Disney Studios)

**Fig. 10-21.** Animation drawing of the Queen from *Snow White and the Seven Dwarfs* (1937). (© Walt Disney Studios)

Fig. 10-22. Gouache cel of Bugs Bunny, circa 1960s, on hand-inked background.

or Courvoisier backgrounds (Courvoisier Galleries was a San Francisco-based firm which sold Disney originals during the 1930s and 1940s through a licensing agreement). Best of all, a piece might have the "matching key production background," resulting in a complete scene as prepared for the camera. These cels are the most coveted—and the most expensive.

There are also cels made just for promotional purposes. These are one-of-a-kind images made for magazines, ads, or packaging that need to look like an authentic scene from the animation of a specific film.

Don't be put off by the fact that some cels are black and white. Like the cartoons from which they come, black-and-white cels are a valued early form of movie memorabilia. In fact, in May of 1990 at Christie's East a black-and-white cel from the Mickey Mouse cartoon *Orphan's Benefit* (1934) sold for $286,000—the highest price paid for any single item of movie memorabilia.

In addition to cels, a number of other novelty items are popular movie collectibles. Buttons featuring film personalities or, given away at movie openings are mass-produced and distributed by the thousands. Some of the more unusual premiere premiums distributed over the years include packets of seeds from *The Invasion of the Body Snatchers,*

**Fig. 10-23.** Three-dimensional animation model of one of the Walking Brooms from *Fantasia* (1940). Made of wood and straw, the model has wire-framed arms that were moved in a variety of positions during animation. (© Walt Disney Studios)

vomit bags from *Airplane II,* Martian money from *Total Recall,* flashlights from *The Gate,* balloons and sunshades from *Jaws: The Revenge,* T-shirts from *Howard the Duck,* and bumper stickers from *The Fog.*

Another item of note is the cigarette card, Hollywood's equivalent of the baseball card. Cigarette cards were produced and distributed in quantity between 1917 and 1937, both in color and in black-and-white. Most cigarette cards measure about 1 1/2″ × 3″, and they could be collected in numbered sets. Each set of 50 cards usually came with an album with space for each card and a capsule biography of the stars. The value of such cards today is $7 to $10 each, depending on the star depicted and the condition of the card.

Some examples of late-1990 values for cels and other items (in mint condition) are given below to give you an idea of the range and variety of values for these items:

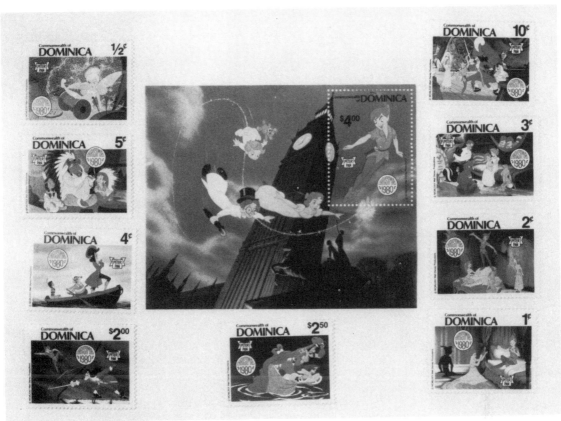

**Fig. 10-24.** A set of postage stamps from Dominica in the West Indies featuring images from *Peter Pan* (1953). (© Walt Disney Studios)

## Cels

Edward G. Robinson and Greta Garbo from "Mother Goose Goes Hollywood" — $3300

Fred Flintstone and Barney Rubble — 460

"Snow White and the Seven Dwarfs" animals in Courvoisier background — 880

"Snow White and the Seven Dwarfs" Dopey and Sleepy in Courvoisier background — 2750

"The Aristocats" Marie and Berlioz — 525

"101 Dalmations" Pongo and Lucky — 850

Tom and Jerry, 1940s — 1600

"Sleeping Beauty" Aurora and forest animals multi-cel setup framed — 1800

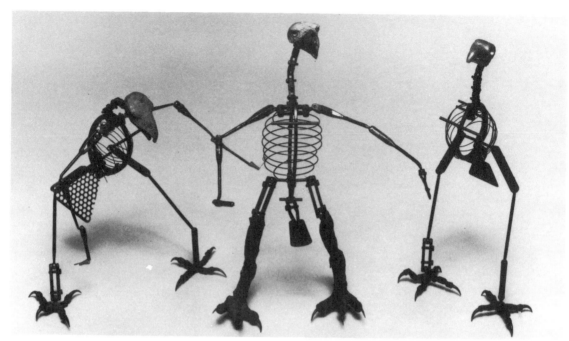

**Fig. 10-25.** Three metal dinosaur armature models used in *One Million Years B.C.* (1937), approximately 14″ × 6″ each.

| | |
|---|---|
| "Little Hiawatha" (1937) Courvoisier background framed and matted, signed by Walt Disney | $1800 |
| Betty Boop, black-and-white | 300 |
| "Cinderella" Gus the Mouse, photo background | 600 |
| "Jungle Book" Shere Khan, framed | 900 |

## Other Items

| | |
|---|---|
| Whip used by Rudolph Valentino in *The Sheik* | $1500 |
| Throne used by Rex Harrison as Julius Caesar in *Cleopatra* | 5000 |
| Three-dimensional animation model of the walking broomstick from *Fantasia* | 8250 |
| Boarman mask from *The Island of Dr. Moreau* | 100 |
| Piano from *Casablanca* | 154,000 |

Autographs, costumes, cels, and novelties appeal to various collectors for various reasons. There is a collecting niche for any movie buff, and many spectacular movie-related collections don't contain a single poster—or any other piece of "standard" movie memorabilia. Collect whatever brings you the most pleasure—that's the cardinal rule of collecting.

Boris Karloff

UNIVERSAL
STAR

**Fig. 10-26.** British cigarette card of Boris Karloff in 1938, 2″ × 1″ (front).

**Fig. 10-27.** Reverse side of card shown in Fig. 10-26.

**Fig. 10-28.** Free movie premiere items: bumper stickers, postcards, frisbees, pins, and 3-D viewer glasses.

# CHAPTER 11

# How to Buy at Auctions and Conventions

**T**HERE ARE MOVIE-RELATED TREASURES hiding in America's attics and basements because collecting movie memorabilia has appealed to people for over four generations. Long-forgotten film items appear every spring at garage sales and flea markets, which means that you can find bits and pieces of Hollywood in your own neighborhood. In addition, specialized movie memorabilia shops are beginning to open up around the country.

Movie memorabilia is becoming part of the popular style and fashion based on nostalgia. Items from the golden age of Hollywood are beautiful in themselves as well as excitingly evocative of the movies and movie personalities with which they are associated.

Most antiques and collectibles shops have available a small number of movie memorabilia curios and knicknacks—perhaps a program book or two, a Mickey Mouse watch, and a few magazines full of old movie advertisements. Because antiques dealers are usually not seriously interested in movie memorabilia as much as they are interested in furniture and glassware, many of them acquire very little of it and do not value it highly. This is good news for movie fans because it means that antiques shops can provide an affordable way of locating and adding new items to a collection of movie memorabilia—if the collector is willing to dig a little.

## Auctions

Another way to acquire authentic movie memorabilia is to buy it directly from the studio, a star's estate, or an established auction house. These opportunities are open to collectors several times each year; ads appear in collectibles publications describing the dates and locations of the events sponsored by such noted auction houses as Sotheby's, Christie's and Camden House. By contacting these organizations prior to the auction, you can

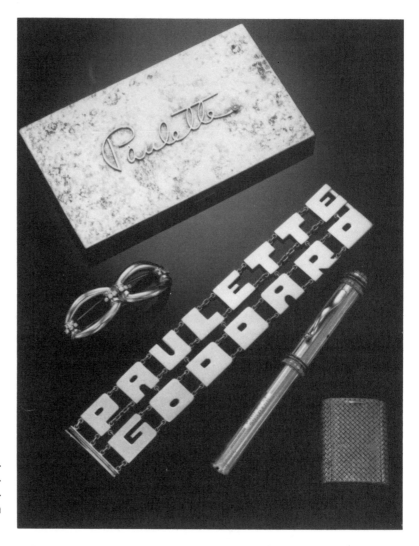

**Fig. 11-1.** A selection of jewelry from the Estate of Paulette Goddard that Sotheby's sold at auction in October 1990.

purchase an illustrated catalog—a collectible in its own right—and learn how to bid on an item or items through the mail.

The Resources section in the back of this book lists the addresses of several auction houses that handle movie memorabilia. And it's possible that you might have something you would wish one of these companies to include in their next auction. If so, you can contact them regarding details of selling an item through their services.

At one of the earliest Hollywood auctions of movie star-related items, in 1945, many of Rudolph Valentino's furnishings from his former home, Falcon's Lair, were offered to the public. There were many sales and auctions of studio properties in the 1950s.

In the 1970s, Twentieth Century-Fox auctioned off decades of extravagant movie memorabilia at what now seem like bargain basement prices. For example, Shirley Tem-

**Fig. 11-2.** This Shirley Temple blue glass pitcher is one of the most common—but also one of the most sought after—Shirley Temple collectibles. It is part of a set that also featured a blue bowl. (Both have been reproduced, so collectors must be alert.)

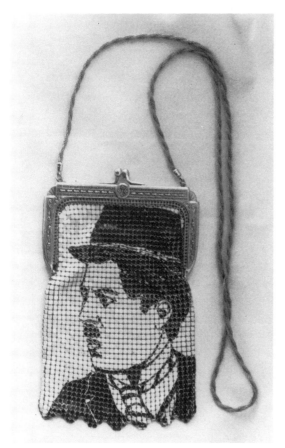

**Fig. 11-3.** This Whiting-David beaded purse featuring Charlie Chaplin in a black-and-white bead motif measures 3 3/4″ × 6″ with a 13 1/2″ chain.

**Fig. 11-4.** A pair of the "ruby" slippers worn by Judy Garland in *The Wizard of Oz* (1939).

ple's toys from *Captain January* (1936) went for $1,065, and Tyrone Power's bed from *Blood and Sand* (1941) fetched $950.

Possibly of more interest to many collectors were the wing chair used in *Laura* (1944), the jeweled mummy case from *Charlie Chan in Egypt* (1935), and the bicycle used in *Butch Cassidy and the Sundance Kid* (1969). All were available for public purchase and went like hotcakes. National attention was brought to these Hollywood auctions when a set of Judy Garland's ruby slippers from *The Wizard of Oz* was sold in the early 1970s for $12,000 (see Fig. 11-4). Less than 20 years later a similar set sold for $165,000. The shoes had been owned by 65-year-old Roberta Bauman, of Memphis, Tennessee. She had kept them in a bank vault, stuffed with cotton and wrapped with towels, since winning them in a contest in 1940 sponsored by MGM. (There was more than one set because comfort and repairs required a backup to this delicate but essential movie prop.)

In the early 1980s, items from the estate of Mary Pickford were auctioned off, including Douglas Fairbank's cape from *The Mark of Zorro* (1920), which sold for $1,800. And a few months later MGM opened its vaults to sell off a remarkable number of items at even more remarkable prices. A Bette Davis dress from *The Old Maid* (1939) was snapped up for $2,200. Sidney Greenstreet's white linen suit from *Across the Pacific* (1942) went for $500, while a leather-bound script from *King Kong* (1933) took in $13,800, and a table lamp from *Gone With the Wind* (1939) fetched over $41,000. The highlight of the sale was the ''Rosebud'' sled from Orson Welles' classic *Citizen Kane* (1941), which went to director Steven Spielberg for $65,000.

Collectors are willing to pay a premium for any jewelry directly identified with a movie star (see Fig. 11-1). The leading auction houses for this kind of material are Christie's, Doyle Galleries, and Sotheby's in New York City, and Butterfield & Butterfield in San Francisco.

Lest you think that all this auction glory is too rich for your blood, here are a few items recently sold through Camden House catalogs at extremely reasonable prices:

- A pale linen gown worn by Virginia Mayo in *The Iron Mistress* (1952)—$200
- A pair of boots worn by Ava Gardner in *Show Boat* (1951)—$150
- An original foam master mold used for masks worn by Vincent Price in *The Abominable Dr. Phibes* (1977)—$125
- Four John Wayne publicity press books from early 1930s westerns—$150
- An artistic double-exposure photo of Marilyn Monroe from an early nude photo session, framed—$125
- Five souvenir programs and one press book from *The Sea Hawk, The Gaucho, Uncle Tom's Cabin, The House of Rothschild, Lloyds of London* and a reissue press book for *Grand Illusion*—$165
- Final shooting script for John Ford–directed film *Four Men and a Prayer* (1938), plus 37 photocopied storyboards—$137
- A ballpoint pen used by Clark Gable to commemorate *Run Silent, Run Deep* (1958)— $220

Such a wealth and variety of props and costumes does not appear frequently on the open market without the assistance of the auction house. Since studios do not keep records of which props were used in specific productions, you must rely on the information provided by the auction house in order to decide for yourself if an item of movie memorabilia is correct or authentic. If you still have doubts about Hollywood auctions, I suggest you contact a few of the auction houses, receive their catalogs and try to discover a more probable way of acquiring movie memorabilia.

# Conventions

Another excellent source of movie memorabilia you might care to look into is film conventions. These are not award ceremonies like the Cannes Film Festival, but rather large gatherings of movie fans like yourself, who meet each year in various parts of the country to watch old films and buy, sell, and trade movie material. (The oldest of these conventions is CINECON, held in a different U.S. city each year over Labor Day weekend.) Movie conventions are great places to meet other collectors, learn what's happening in the field, see the latest movie-related items, and buy lots of old and rare movie memorabilia.

When you first arrive at a convention, pause before you buy anything. Take your time to carefully inspect the items you're eager to buy. Ask the seller to hold them for you for up to an hour; usually this is no problem for the seller, and it lets you test yourself and see if you really want to buy the material. The waiting period also gives you time to check out the other dealers to see if you can find another copy of the same lobby card, cartoon, or whatever at a lower price.

There are other advantages to waiting before buying when you're attending a film convention. You should wait before deciding to buy any item simply because it gains you the only power you have as a buyer other than the power of money—*time*. Time is to your advantage, because there are so many opportunities to purchase materials at a convention that it's somewhat a buyer's market. You might work up a deal with vendor #1 and put it on hold to work up a different deal with vendor #2. Perhaps then you can even go back to #1 and get an extra item that #2 needs, thus improving your chances for a good deal with #2.

Another reason to wait is that many dealers don't want to pack everything up at the end of the convention and lug all their movie material home. To avoid this chore, they will have a "going out of business" sale. On the last day of a convention, you can usually find several dealers who will sell their wares at rock-bottom prices. When this happens, you'll be glad you held back some of your money to wait for these bargains.

Finally, when you conclude your deal and get ready to leave a dealer's table, wait again. Double-check to be sure you have everything you should: the memorabilia you just bought, any other items you were holding (including your wallet), and the correct change. All the excitement and chaos of a film convention will often distract you from these important things, and it'll be almost impossible to go back even after a few minutes and try to find or explain what you've lost or forgotten. There's no reward for buying fast. Take your time and do things right.

Here are a few more tips that will improve your experiences at a movie convention:

- *Before you go to a convention, get your want list polished.* Believe me, when you're there, you'll see hundreds of tempting buys. There will be so many tantalizing items that you'll soon lose sight of what items you are looking for unless you can refer to a prearranged list of the posters, autographs, films, and books you desire most.

- *Get there early.* If you wait until the second day of the convention, many of the choice deals will already have been snapped up. You want to be there when the doors open so you can inspect the best copies of your favorite one-sheets and seek out the best price. Remember, the greater the selection, the better your chances of finding the specific pieces of memorabilia you seek. So get there early when the selection is the greatest.

- *Never buy at the dealer's first price.* A movie convention is not a supermarket where everything is priced or marked down. If you want a discount, you will have to ask for it. Consider inspecting the grade and condition of an item out loud—sometimes the dealer will volunteer a lower price, if you just inquire about the condition of the print or magazine.

- *Never leave your own items sitting out where a dealer or another attendee can mistake them for their own.* It's a good idea to come to the convention with a carrying case of some sort that contains your name and address so you can easily reclaim your materials if they are lost.

- *Never be tempted to steal.* A movie convention may look like a lot of chaos, but it is not. Dealers know their wares, and they know how to protect them. No item is worth the shame and embarrassment you'll suffer if you try to rip someone off. You expect to get a fair deal, and you should expect to give one, too.

- *Meet as many guests as you can.* These people are there to give you an insight into the creative side of Hollywood. You can learn a lot about what it's like to be involved with a motion picture, if you politely ask questions. You'll be amazed to find that many people who are involved with the business of motion pictures collect movie memorabilia, too.

- *At the end of the convention, take stock of the material you've purchased.* Inspect everything a second time and try to recall which dealer or collector you got it from. If you discover any defects, hold on to the original bag, tag, and wrappings to prove that the memorabilia came from a specific dealer. Usually, you'll have no trouble returning an item, assuming that there is a genuine problem with it. Convention dealers are just as conscious of their good image as are the owners of local movie memorabilia shops.

After attending a few conventions, you might get the idea to set up a table yourself. No problem. It's easy to know in advance when a convention is scheduled in your area. Check the listings in the *The Big Reel* and the ads in *Classic Images* and *Movie Collectors World* for the dates and locations of the upcoming cinema conventions nearest you. Many of the more popular conventions are listed in the Resources section of this book. And more information on conventions and auctions is contained in Chapter 3.

# CHAPTER 12

# Taking Care of Your Collection

**C**OLLECTIBLES IN ALL AREAS are becoming popular investments in America, for both nostalgic and supply-and-demand reasons. Most collectibles today are once-ordinary items that have become scarce because of deterioration and destruction. A collectible is worth something only if it remains in good condition.

Years ago, it was fine to buy magazines and records for their enjoyment alone; after a while no one cared if the kids played with them. But this is no longer the case since many "ordinary items" have now become collectibles.

Few collectors realize, however, that as their goodies are gaining value they are also deteriorating, even if the kids aren't doing a job on them. The elements of the erosive environment are the culprits, slowly eating away at our investments. But with proper care and safe storage of collectibles, the life of these valuable items can be extended considerably.

## Preservation

The fatal mistake many collectors make is to spend all of their money on the collection and none on preservation. The time to act is now, rather than after it's too late.

Ignorance or disregard for the natural laws of aging and deterioration will eventually result in the destruction of your movie memorabilia, making remaining similar items owned by other collectors who have taken proper care worth all that much more. A collection of movie memorabilia is a great source of enjoyment, and the protection of your collection will also make it a sound investment over time—instead of a pile of dust.

You must do your best to protect your posters, lobbies, and stills from the ravages of time, light, pollution, humidity, heat, water, acid, and pests. Talk to a good picture framer, read a book, or visit the conservation department of your local museum to supplement the information on preservation given below.

**Fig. 12-1.** *Movie Classic* magazine (August 1935) with cover illustration of Dolores Del Rio.

Paper memorabilia items can suffer permanent damage if stored in damp basements (they get moldy), hot attics (they get dried out and brittle), or in garages (they get eaten by critters). The best place to store your collection is in a cool, dry room away from direct sunlight and the ultraviolet effects of fluorescent lighting.

If you can't find a room where the temperature is a constant 65°F, then at least be sure that the air is dehumidified. Dehumidification will retard the decay that occurs due to the acidic nature of the cheap paper. If you can't avoid windows or fluorescent light, at least put up some block-out curtains and ultraviolet block shields on the overhead lights. These efforts, too, will keep the paper from yellowing and becoming brittle.

Fig. 12-2. George Hurrell photograph of Joan Crawford.

Eventually you may discover that your collection has become so large that storing it without damage is a problem. One of the best investments you can make is in proper storage materials, that is, plastic bags, plastic sleeves and special storage boxes. You can purchase these supplies from many sources. Two of the leaders in mail-order storage paraphernalia are Bill Cole Enterprises (P.O. Box 60, Randolph, MA 02368) and Friendly Frank's Distribution (3990 Broadway, Gary, IN 46408). Write to them for any of the items discussed below.

You should consider purchasing a supply of 3-mil polyethylene bags for placement on each record album, poster, and magazine. These bags prevent damage from dirt, moisture, and other dangerous elements that unprotected items are subjected to. But be

Fig. 12-3. Before and after views of reconditioned one-sheet poster from *That Hamilton Woman* (1941).

aware that this type of plastic is unstable and can trap the acid from the paper in the bag, thus cooking your movie materials in their own juices. If you use polyethylene bags, don't tape them shut. Paper and plastics need to "breathe."

Also available are the special storage boxes mentioned above, which physically protect your collection from light, trauma, and critters and also provide a small degree of deacidification. Deacidification can counter for many years the effects of the acidic content of rag paper. Over time, this acidic content will cause the paper to yellow, then brown, and finally become brittle and crumble to dust. You've probably seen this happen to old newspapers that have been left piled up in storage. With deacidification, most of these deteriorating effects can be stopped.

One of the best items you can buy to help preserve your collection is a supply of Mylar bags. These tough, clear-plastic envelopes are strong enough to stand your lobbies up on end, and they give off no chemical vapors over time. These bags can make even a faded and soiled poster look great. Mylar bags also mean you don't need to purchase cardboard sheets or backing board to place in each bag as a stiffener. This will save you several cents per item and help cover the expense of the Mylar.

Fig. 12-4. Before and after views of reconditioned one-sheet poster from *When Ladies Meet* (1941).

# Repairs

All this bagging and boxing might at first seem like a lot of work, but compared to other hobbies, collecting and preserving most movie memorabilia is practically no trouble at all. The real trouble comes when you try to repair or restore a damaged collectible.

On a valuable poster, it is sometimes better to accept the defect and live with it, rather than try to repair or hide it. If the poster is not valuable, you can attempt to repair it yourself, knowing that the time and effort will probably not pay you back by elevating the item's condition to a higher grade. In other words, your attempts to repair a piece of movie memorabilia may make it look better and be more appealing to you but will probably not make it more valuable.

Don't attempt repairs or restorations on your own. Don't dry-mount a poster or use Scotch tape anywhere on the poster. Scotch tape has an oil-based adhesive that over time will stain the paper, making it almost transparent, like wax paper. Use acid-free tape when tape is required. A thick tape will help reinforce the folds in a poster.

Do not attempt to remove the folds from movie posters, since the folds are part of

**Fig. 12-5.** Before and after views of reconditioned one-sheet poster from *The Mark of Zorro* (1940).

the printing process and do not detract from the value of the poster unless there is damage or tears at the folds. The most serious damage is actual missing pieces, particularly when those pieces are in the main artwork. Serious fold damage, missing pieces, and so on can reduce the value of a poster from 35 to 65 percent.

Don't try to use a magic marker or ballpoint pen to do artistic retouching. These sorts of inks will eventually spread into the paper, leaving a stainlike discoloration. Also, never use a marker or pen to price a poster on the backside; the ink will sink through to the other side over the years.

Storing posters, magazines, and photos out of direct sunlight will prevent fading. Some collectors frame their posters, while others use transparent plastic bags to hold lobby cards and folded one-sheets. Rolled posters are less likely to be damaged as long as the edges have not been bent.

If a favorite poster is beginning to self-destruct, it is time to mount it on linen. This traditional and expensive method of preservation does not lessen poster value and is reversible. Consider having this done by an expert.

Linen mounting of a poster is not really mounting on linen per se but rather double mounting. The poster is fixed to 10 percent cotton duck with an inner layer of Japanese

**Fig. 12-6.** Before and after views of reconditioned one-sheet poster from *The Philadelphia Story* (1940).

*okawara,* which is acid-free rice paper. The rice paper helps compensate for the difference between the expansion coefficients for the poster paper and the cotton duck. Usually professionals guarantee their work but not the behavior of the varieties of old and unstable paper they are asked to work with. Wrinkles and crumpled paper is laid smooth, tears are repaired, missing pieces are restored and repainted.

Lobby cards and inserts, which are usually printed on heavier card stock, are treated differently. The edges (especially if they've been trimmed to fit inside a frame) may need to be rematched with paper from a different lobby card, but one that is from the same era, studio, and color.

Corners can become bent, or holes can be torn out. In this case, inlays of similar paper can be put in. For example, if you have the right and left halves of a lobby card, it is better to reconstruct two new ones than to throw out parts and only make one new one. This is because a restored piece of paper memorabilia is worth almost 100 percent of its normal value. When it comes time to sell, you should advise a buyer that you've had the work restored, but it shouldn't make much difference in price.

Expect to have to do lots of retouching of the paint and ink on most old, poorly

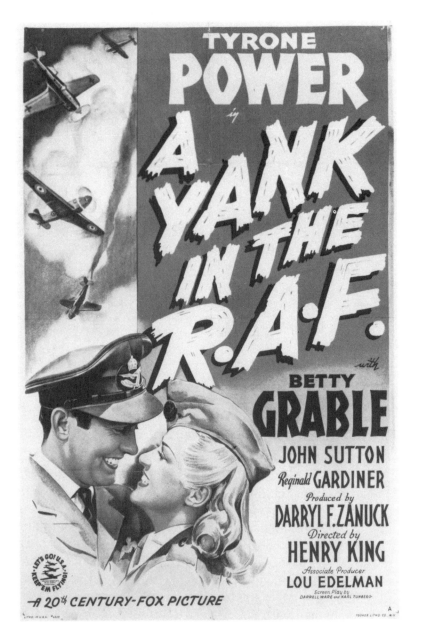

**Fig. 12-7.** One-sheet poster from *A Yank in the R.A.F.* (1941).

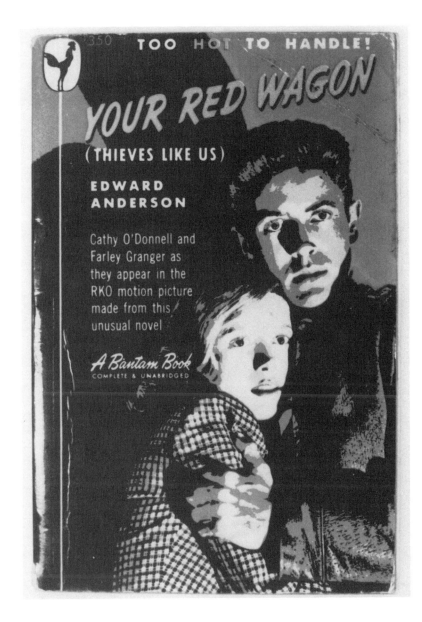

**Fig. 12-8.** Paperback novel *Thieves Like Us* in its movie edition *Your Red Wagon* (1948).

maintained paper memorabilia. Entire sections of a torn or chipped poster may need to be repainted into place. Perhaps it's the high demand and low supply of classic movie posters that makes this an acceptable practice.

Typical prices for these services are $1 per inch along the longest dimension of the poster. For example, a 40″ × 30″ poster would be $40. Stain removal is usually half this amount, as is the cost of removing any old backing. Paint and ink touchup is likely to be near $20 per hour. Businesses that perform this service will ship throughout the United

**Fig. 12-9.** One-sheet poster for *My Gal Sal* (1942).

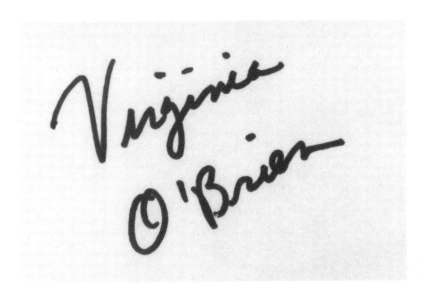

**Fig. 12-10.** Autograph of Virginia O'Brien.

States via insured or registered mail. Return postage costs are additional. One of the best practitioners of this "art form" is Crowell Beech, who can be reached at Gone Hollywood, 172 Bella Vista Ave., Belvedere, CA 94920.

# Organization

The best thing you can do for your collection is to take care of it and keep track of it. If you have all your movie memorabilia organized for quick and easy reference, you can locate each item with a minimum of handling. When you cut down handling, you cut down wear and tear. And in order to do this, you need to have some sort of organized method of filing and finding individual items.

The basic way to keep track of your collection is to log every item you own into either a hand-written file-card system or a computer program. There are advantages to each.

The file-card system is simple and effective. This system has the further advantage of providing you with a handy want list to use while at conventions or movie collectibles shops.

An inventory computer program has the advantage of easily listing many more fields of data than can fit on a simple file card. You can set up your own program from a data-management system, or you can purchase one of the preprogrammed discs available from several software vendors. The computerized system of tracking your collection lets you enter and recall such additional fields of data as original cost, current market price, sale price, and quantity. If you plan on investing heavily in movie memorabilia, I would recommend that you begin computerizing your collection now. Then, as you buy, sell, and speculate, you can easily scan and sort through tons of data to see which investments have paid off and which transactions have gained you a good profit.

**Fig. 12-11.** Autographed edition of *E.T. The Extraterrestrial Storybook* signed by the cast, crew, and executives of the film, including Steven Spielberg, Dee Wallace, Drew Barrymore, and John Williams.

Taking care of and keeping track of your movie memorabilia is the first step in evolving from a casual film fan into a serious collector or dealer. But even if you never want to sell any pieces from your collection, you probably want to keep it for as long as you can. If you follow the suggestions I've presented in this chapter, there's no reason why you can't enjoy all of your movie memorabilia for as long as you like.

# CHAPTER 13

# How to Price and Sell Memorabilia

**W**HETHER YOU HAVE BEEN BUILDING your collection for a few years or for only a few months, sooner or later there will probably come a time when you will decide to sell some of your movie memorabilia. There are many reasons for selling items from a collection. Perhaps the attraction of a particular piece has worn off, or maybe you'd like to sell some minor items to enable you to get a more expensive item. There are those who tire of collecting altogether and sell an entire collection, and there are noncollectors who, while cleaning the attic, stumble onto some bit of Hollywood history they have no wish to keep. Whatever your reasons for selling, you will find a variety of ways to go about it.

I knew when I bought my first movie memorabilia—a set of lobby cards from *The Bride of Frankenstein* (1935)—that it was worth much more than the small amount of money I paid for it. Don't ask me how I knew; I could just "feel" it. And that feeling is the beginning and end of calculating what your collectibles are worth.

Most collectors these days automatically refer to one or more of the available price guides to quickly and easily figure the value of their memorabilia. But before you do that, ask yourself what each item is worth to you personally. Do you "feel" as if this particular soundtrack is better than most? If so, then it's "worth" more to you than most other soundtracks, and you should think twice about selling it. Many times, the feeling is like that which you have for an old friend or a favorite toy; to other people it means little, but to you it means a lot.

Have you noticed how many times I've placed words in quotation marks throughout the last few paragraphs? I've done this because I'm not talking about agreed-upon or established things. I'm talking about perception—your perception of a "valuable item" versus someone else's perception of a "pile of old junk."

When it comes to placing a value on your collection, your perception will be different from anyone else's. This is because these are *your* collectibles, the ones you've saved

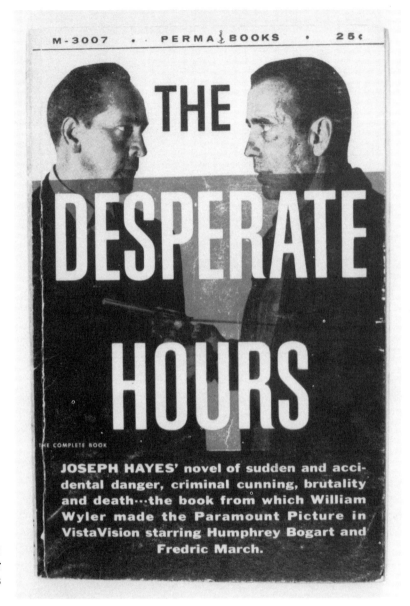

Fig. 13-1. Paperback novel *The Desperate Hours* as it was issued during the film's release.

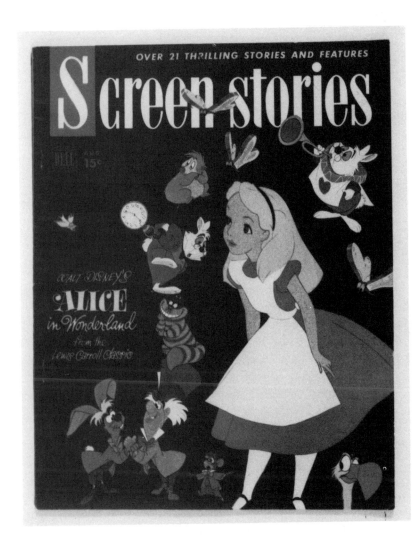

and looked after and liked. Your first impression is that they are very valuable. When you notice the prices listed in an ad or price guide, often you feel as if you were right all along to feel as if your movie memorabilia was worth a lot of money. That's nice, but what good does it do you?

Once in a while, you'll be surprised to find that a film or a piece of related memorabilia you liked very much is listed in a price guide as being worth very little. The reason is probably supply and demand. Is your perception wrong? No, it's just different.

## Basic Values

In the next few paragraphs I'm going to show you three different ways to place a value on many of your movie collectibles, all based on different perceptions. But remember that the true value of any collectible is always based on your own perception. If you like it, if it brings joy to you, if it is the perfect example in your mind of a wonderful movie poster or set of lobby cards—then it's worth more than any guide listing suggests. It's priceless, and you should consider hanging onto it regardless of its accepted "value."

The *salvage price* of movie memorabilia is the price someone will pay you for the bulk paper or plastic on which your collection is imprinted. Obviously, this buyer has no perception of collectibles beyond that of their recyclable elments. If you sell your collection at the salvage price, you will get quick cash, little discussion, and low money.

The *buy price* of an item is the price commonly advertised by dealers who seek collectibles at a rate that will allow them to pay you quickly and cover their overhead expenses. This price is usually about 50 percent of the properly graded guide price, but sometimes it can be a little more, if the dealer or collector shares your perception that your memorabilia is special or better-than-average. The *buy price* assures you a lengthy discussion and inspection of each item and, in many cases, a longer payment period.

The *guide price* of a collectible is the price listed in various price guides or in publication advertisements. It represents the selling or asking price commonly agreed upon by most dealers. Of course, you know that you can usually find collectibles for less than guide price and also that dealers need to make some money when they go to sell your items, so it's reasonable to expect that you'll be asked to sell your items at prices below those listed in the guides. Still, you usually can get something close to the guide price if you sell or trade your items to another collector. This is because other collectors usually share your perception of the value of movie memorabilia—and because they're not concerned with overhead and profit, as dealers are. Unless your tastes are uneducated or are completely out of line with the tastes of most movie fans, you can expect the guide price to give you a respectable return and a long discussion with other collectors. And what's so bad about that?

A final word about the guide price. You should think of it as a reference for *trading* materials, not buying or selling. Since there are so many different types of movie memorabilia and so many perceptions of worth, the guide price is a guide to help you swap a lot of record albums or posters with a minimum of argument.

# The Rule of One-Half

Even with movie items that are 80 years old, you have to buy them at retail prices and sell at wholesale. For example, suppose you buy an old issue of *Photoplay* for $50 from a dealer. If you read the magazine and try to sell it back to the dealer the next month, he or she will probably be able to buy it back from you for only $25. This is the *Rule of One-Half:* You can sell an item to a dealer for about one-half of the price at which you can buy that same item (or a similar one) from the same dealer.

Another way to look at it is that in order to recoup your initial investment, you're going to have to wait until the *Photoplay* issue is worth at least $100 retail before you can sell it for the $50 wholesale that you originally paid. This means you should view your collectibles as long-term investments, since the average appreciation of most movie

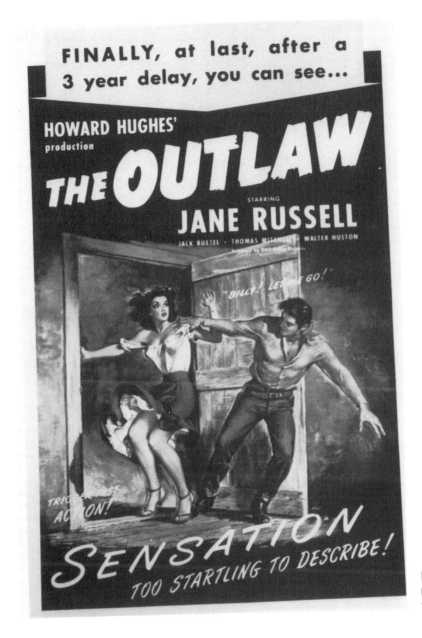

Fig. 13-3. From *The Outlaw* (1943) a one-sheet poster featuring Jane Russell.

items is only 10 percent per year. That equates to a waiting period of roughly 10 years before you break even.

However, keep in mind that most videotapes will never be worth more than what you paid for them. And most 16mm and 8mm films have stabilized in value since the market demand for these visual stories has been filled by videotapes and videodiscs.

A note about the values in this book: I have used information from dealer surveys and catalogs and auctions to compile the price estimates, but in the end I am responsible for what you read here. Most vintage movie posters tend to appreciate at a rate of 10 to 20 percent per year. Generally, bad economic times will depress this rate and the death of a major star or sudden rise to fame of an actor depicted might elevate this rate. Imagine the recent change in value of an autograph given by Sammy Davis, Jr., or Jim Henson— values go way up because the source of supply is gone. Also, fads are just that: fads. For example, it once was very popular to collect items associated with animation designer Ray Harryhausen, but the technology of this art has passed beyond Harryhausen's style, and interest in his films has waned. B-westerns are currently very popular, but the number of fans of this type of film are shrinking yearly, and this lessening popularity will soon affect values and prices.

# Ways to Sell Your Memorabilia

There are many ways to sell your movie memorabilia. Some are quick and make you very little profit. Others are long, drawn-out affairs that can give you a good return on your investment.

Outside of someone walking up and knocking on your door, asking to buy your movie memorabilia at top dollar (Would you ever sell your favorite treasures, even under these conditions?), the best time to sell is when you're not in the mood and not in need of money. When you're not in a hurry to sell your items, you will hold back until the deal is strongly in your favor. A dealer does this because to the dealer the sale of movie material is necessary income, but not income that should be realized at a financial sacrifice (hence, the Rule of One-Half).

Try to keep your *need* to sell your memorabilia at a minimum so you won't be tempted to let items go at below-value prices. As with buying, if you can control your desire to rush through a deal, you stand a good chance to improve the deal in your favor. So how can you casually sell your collectibles? There are at least four ways of selling your memorabilia that will require a bit of effort but will get you a good return. These are discussed in the next several sections.

## Selling at a Convention

You can, of course, sign up to operate a dealer's table at many of the cinema conventions held across the country every year. Check the Resources section of this book or check current issues of the three movie memorabilia newspapers for the addresses, dates, and locations of these multi-day meetings. Conventions are very popular and busy events, and you should contact the convention managers at least four months in advance in order to rent table space in the dealers room. The rate for renting a table can range from $20 to $150 per table, depending on the size of the convention's attendance, and will often net you a free admission to the convention, too.

Working a table can be a lot of fun, but it is also just what you might think: *work.*

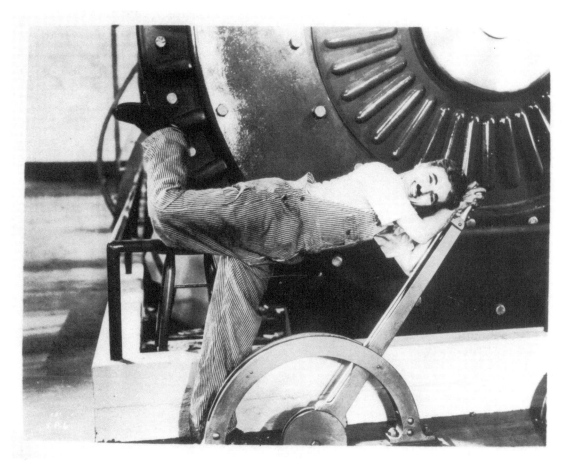

**Fig. 13-4.** Still of Charlie Chaplin from *Modern Times* (1936).

To begin with, you must have your material organized so that customers can find what they're searching for. To protect the condition of your items, you'll need a set of boxes to display your lobbies, soundtracks, and books. Individual bags and backing boards will help keep things in tip-top shape. And you'll have to lug them all into the convention hall early in the morning so you'll be set up and ready for business when the doors open.

You can expect to be asked a lot of questions about the movie memorabilia you have for sale. Customers will want to know where things are and if you have a specific item or items related to their favorite film star or director. This means you'll need to know just what it is you're selling. And, of course, you'll need to make the correct change, to keep an eye on all your wares, and to try to work several deals at once with the droves of customers who want to buy your memorabilia.

You are free to discount your material as much as you like, whenever you like. Also you might find that another dealer will be interested in buying up, say, all the movie magazines you have left at the end of the convention, for a hefty discount. One of the advantages of selling your leftovers this way is that you don't have to bother to pack things up when the convention is over.

But the best advice for being a dealer is the same as for being a customer: *Take your time.* Don't panic or allow yourself to be stampeded by the demands of the attendees.

## Selling on Consignment Through a Dealer

In consignment sales, you allow a dealer to keep your items in the dealer's store or take them to a convention in the hope that the dealer will be able to sell the items for you. Because the dealer is not actually buying your materials, you don't get paid until a customer pays the dealer. But since you are using the dealer's site to improve your product's exposure to the mass market, you should expect to pay the dealer a small percentage, or carrying fee, out of each sale.

The risks of consignment sales are that your materials may not sell for some time (or at all); that they may be damaged while on display; that the dealer will perhaps not try very hard to sell your items; and that the dealer won't report honestly the final sale price.

You can minimize these risks by working out a written agreement that includes the following points:

- Detailed description of all items
- Sale price
- Responsibility for loss or damage
- Length of time of consignment
- Date of payment

Be sure the agreement is dated and signed by both parties. You each then keep a copy, and the dealer does all the work while you reap most of the rewards.

## Selling Through Auctions

Movie memorabilia auctions are regularly advertised in the three movie newspapers, as well as in many antique and collectible publications. Auction houses across the country stand ready to accept your movie material on consignment for inclusion in future auctions. An auction house will work with you to help determine an estimated price range for your items. You may also establish a ''reverse'' price which is a minimum price below which the auction house will not sell your piece. The main advantage of sale through an auction house is that your memorabilia is exposed to a bidding process. If two or more people are interested in your autograph, poster, or soundtrack, they will bid the price up until only one interested party remains.

**Fig. 13-5.** Autograph matted with color photo of Walt Disney; 21″ × 32″.

There are some disadvantages associated with auctions. Because of the popularity of auctions and the infrequency with which they are conducted, the auction houses are presented with a quantity of materials that far exceeds their maximum capacity for any given sale. As a result, the auction houses have become increasingly selective in accepting materials.

Then, too, there can be quite a few costs associated with placing an item in auction. In some cases a seller is expected to pay the auction house between 10 and 20 percent of the final bid. Additionally, auction houses may charge miscellaneous fees for such things as photography, insurance, and handling. Finally, in supplying your material to the auction house, you must understand that it is being handled by many different people without your supervision. While precautions are taken, damage to items has been known to occur.

When you begin discussing an auction sale ask about the commission. Is it a flat rate or a sliding scale? What other costs will you incur? Insurance? Shipping? When will the sale be held? When will it be over? When will payment be made? What is the fee, if any, for the service? Usually, all this is covered in the auctioneer's contract, so be sure to ask to review a copy before you make a commitment.

As with consignment sales to stores, the main disadvantage to selling your movie memorabilia through an auction is the comparatively long time between the day you consign the items and the day of the auction, followed by the time between the sale and the receipt of payment.

## Running an Ad

The easiest and most profitable way to sell your items is to buy space in one or more of the movie memorabilia newspapers and run an ad offering your items directly to other collectors all across the country. State the name, condition, and price of the items, and sit back to wait for the telephone to ring. The easiest method of covering the shipping and handling charges is to build them into the selling price. This makes your ad simple to write and read, and you don't have to worry about buyers forgetting to include these charges in their payments.

Be sure to include your telephone number so collectors can call and reserve items before their cash arrives. Also, ask collectors to list alternates when they respond to your ad; if two people send money for the same poster or autograph, you'll be glad you did. Tell your buyers to include something like $2 or $3 for postage and insurance if you don't build those costs into your prices, and also specify a minimum order amount ($5 to $10) so you won't spend days wrapping and sending out small orders.

Be sure to specify that payment be made via money orders or certified check, unless you are willing to wait several weeks to see if a buyer's personal check clears your bank. Expect to have to take back a few of the items you've sold, just because of the difference in perception of grading between you and your buyer. Refund the money quickly and without hassle; you can always sell the material later.

**Fig. 13-6.** Classic window card of *China Seas* (1935) featuring Clark Gable, Jean Harlow, and Wallace Beery.

A variation of this direct sales technique might help you sell your entire collection at once. Assemble a list of dealers from the various ads you find in price guides and other publications and do a mass mailing of your list with prices to these potential buyers. Remember to state the proper grading or condition of each item in the collection. Break the list of items down into lots and assign each lot a special lot price. It's also a good

Fig. 13-7. Autographed candid photo from the 1940s of actor Boris Karloff.

idea to give a low "one price takes all," in the hopes of selling everything to one dealer in one shipment.

If you receive a response in the form of an offer, wrap the items up and ship them off to the dealer. The dealer's offer letter as a response to your original list constitutes an agreement. After your materials arrive and the dealer has had a few weeks to verify the content and grading, you should receive a check for the offered amount. If you haven't heard anything in three weeks, it's time to place a polite but firm telephone call.

The secret of selling well is the same as the secret of buying well: Don't worry about possessing an item forever. Enjoy the item while you have it, and move on to bigger and better things when it's time.

# Afterword

**T**HE FUTURE IS BRIGHT for collecting movie memorabilia. The promotion and hype of new items and newly available old items will continue to draw attention to movie memorabilia from nearly all age groups. Each year, more and more movie shops open in the United States and more and more collectors come into the market. The thrill of the product is perfect for impulse buying and the adventure of American shopping. And, if you pay careful attention to smart buying and selling—and you really love movie memorabilia—you just might become the owner of one of these entertaining and popular movie memorabilia stores.

Recent successful trends in the presentation of popular television and feature films suggest a rosy future for movie material. Big-budget adventure films with lots of eye-popping special effects stimulate the average viewer to want more items connected with the fun and entertainment. Skilled animation studios have created an increased interest from the children's market. Summer block-busters, holiday features, and made-for-TV films all indicate that movies—and movie memorabilia—are an integral part of our culture and will continue to be so in times to come. New collecting tools and reference volumes—like this book—are coming into the market every year.

Given the continual popularity of movies and the memorabilia that they spawn, demand for movie-related collectibles will most likely continue to increase. But whether it increases or not, there is one thing you can be certain of: Collecting movie memorabilia will always be fun and exciting!

# Sources of Additional Information

## Movie Memorabilia Auctions

Camden House
10921 Wilshire Blvd., Suite 808
Los Angeles, CA 90024
(213) 476-1628

Christie's
219 E. 67th St.
New York, NY 10021
(212) 606-0560

Doyle Auctioneers
137 Osborne Hill Rd.
Fishkill, NY 12524
(914) 896-9492

Guernsey's
136 E. 73 St.
New York, NY 10021
(212) 794-2280

Hake's Americana
P.O. Box 1444
York, PA 17405

Sotheby's
1334 York Ave.
New York, NY 10021

## Movie Memorabilia Shops and Dealers

### California

Cinema Collectors
1507 Wilcox Ave.
Hollywood, CA 90028
(213) 461-6516

Collectors Bookstore
1708 N. Vine St.
Hollywood, CA 90028
(213) 467-3296

Framex
4054 Laurel Canyon Blvd.
Studio City, CA 91604
(818) 509-0700

Gone Hollywood
172 Bella Vista Ave.
Belvedere, CA 94920
(415) 435-1929

Hollywood Book and Poster Co.
1706 N. Las Palmas Ave.
Hollywood, CA 90028
(213) 465-8764

Hollywood Book City Collectibles
6631 Hollywood Blvd.
Los Angeles, CA 90028
(213) 466-1020

Hollywood Memories
Port of Call Village
Berth 76, Store W-8
San Pedro, CA 90731
(213) 548-4423

La Belle Epoque
1111 Gayley Ave.
Los Angeles, CA 90024
(213) 208-8449

Larry Edmunds Book Shop
6658 Hollywood Blvd.
Los Angeles, CA 90028
(213) 463-3273

Last Moving Picture Co.
6307 Hollywood Blvd.
Hollywood, CA 90028

Movie Memories Poster Shop
502 Waverly St.
Palo Alto, CA 94301
(415) 328-6265

Movie Posters
8961 Mint Ave.
Westminister, CA 92683
(714) 841-1314

## Georgia

The Paper Chase
4073 LaVista Rd. Suite 363
Tucker, GA 30084
(800) 433-0025

## Minnesota

Grand Slam
3017 Lyndale Ave. S.
Minneapolis, MN 55408
(612) 823-3174

## Nevada

Hollywood Movie Posters
900 E. Karen, Suite 215-B
Las Vegas, NV 89109
(702) 735-8170

## New York

Jerry Ohlinger's Movie Material
242 W. 14th Street
New York, NY 10011
(212) 989-0869

## Ohio

Jack's Collectibles
8761 Smokey Row Rd.
Powell, OH 43065
(614) 792-1722

Last Moving Picture Co.
2044 Euclid Ave.
Cleveland, OH 44115
(216) 781-1821

Manuscript Investments
Conover Plaza
654 Brice Rd.
Reynoldsburg, OH 43068
(614) 866-9000

Movie Madness
Clarion Hotel Skywalk
Cincinnati, OH 45202
(513) 241-9856

## Tennessee

Luton's Poster Exchange
2780 Frayser Blvd. Suite D
Memphis, TN 38127
(901) 357-1649

# Collector Supplies

Bags Unlimited
53 Canal St. Dept. D
Rochester, NY 14608
(716) 436-9006

# Animation Cels

Art to Cel
6161 28th St. S.E.
Grand Rapids, MI 49546
(616) 940-3665

Character Builders
681 S. High St.
Worthington, OH 43085

Cricket Gallery
529 Covington Place
Wyckoff, NJ 07481
(800) BUY-CELS

# Cinema Conventions

## March

Cinefest/Syracuse
215 Dawly Rd.
Fayetteville, NY 13066
(315) 637-8985

## May

Cinevent/Columbus
380 South 5th St.
Columbus, OH 43215

## June

Big D Super Collectibles Show
Box 111266
Arlington, TX 76007
(817) 261-8745

Western Film Fair
1508 Prisma Court
Raleigh, NC 27612
(919) 782-9320

Nostalgia USA's Film Festival
Suite 2309
100 N. Main Bldg.
Memphis, TN 38103

## August

Fanex
Box 6220
Baltimore, MD 21206
(301) 665-1198

Memphis Film Festival
P.O. Box 40272
Memphis, TN 38174

## September

Cinecon
978 S. Murfield Rd.
Los Angeles, CA 90019
(213) 937-0776

October

Atlanta Film Fair
2289 S. Cobb Dr. S.E.
Smyrna, GA 30080
(404) 434-8887

# Publications

The Big Reel
Empire Publishing
Route #3 Box 83
Madison, NC 27025

Classic Images
P.O. Box 809
Muscatine, WI 52761

Filmfax
1042 1/2 Michigan Ave.
Evanston, IL 60202

Movie Collector's World
P.O. Box 309
Fraser, MI 48026

# Autographs

Courts
3020 Lake Arnold Place
Orlando, FL 32806
(407) 897-6850

Hurd's Outpost
5108 Hoagland Blockstub
Courtland, OH 44410
(216) 638-7215

# Poster and Lobby Card Reproductions

Archival Photography
14845 Anne St.
Allen Park, MI 48101
(313) 388-5452

# Laser Discs

Ken Crone's Laser Disc
14260 Beach Blvd.
Westminister, CA 92683
(800) 624-3078

Sight and Sound
1275 Main St.
Waltham, MA 02154
(617) 894-8633

# Videotapes

American Entertainment International
1–3 Union St.
Dover-Foxcroft, Maine 04426

Chiller Theatre Video
P.O. Box 2608
Bloomfield, NJ 07003
(201) 507-8458

Foothill Video
P.O. Box 547
Tujunga, CA 91042
(818) 353-8591

Sinister Cinema
P.O. Box 777
Pacifica, CA 94044

# Films

Boopzilla
54 Turner St. #3
Brighton, MA 02135
(617) 783-3691

Capt. Bijou
P.O. Box 87
Toney, AL 35773
(205) 852-0198

Modern Sound Pictures Inc.
1402 Howard St.
Omaha, NE 68102
(402) 341-8476

National Cinema Service
P.O. Box 43
Ho-Ho-Kus, NJ 07423
(201) 445-0776

Thornhill Entertainment
2143-E Stateville Blvd.
Suite 168
Salisbury, NC 28144
(704) 636-1116

# Magazines

Ron Andrus
224 Lantern Dr., N.W.
Comstock Park, MI 49321
(616) 784-5949

# Scripts

California Script
8033 Sunset Blvd.
Suite 394
Hollywood, CA 90046
(213) 460-2535

# Index